"Jacobs masterfully unfolds t[...] pervasive and powerful influen[...] as well as those who benefit fro[...] book are chapters from my own life, allowing me to further explore my own pain, struggle, curiosity, and courage. If you're serious about unpacking the often-avoided topic of racism, then I highly encourage you to read this book!"

— Lawrence Garrett
Owner and Chief Impact Officer at 828 Flow
and author of *The Equity Starter Kit*

"This book centers racial learning and it delivers. It is conversational, candid, and practical. The compelling narrative plays out just as it does in our heads, in our relationships, in our organizations, and in the streets. This book is a powerful resource to study and share so we can have courageous conversations with our colleagues. We should convene the conference that this book envisions!"

— Chuck Shelton
Chief Executive Officer at Greatheart Consulting

"*The Elephant in the Room* is like being a 'fly on the wall' and listening to a captivating snippet from the longest, quietest, most threatening conversation everyone's having and no one's listening to: the race conversation in corporate America. This book's conversational narrative begs readers to sense both familiarity and discomfort as it intimates the hidden emotions and secret toll race stokes for every person in the workplace. Jacobs' characters remind us that we all have impact, and meaningful change can be born from boldly listening to the power behind real and raw conversations about race."

— Kipepo Brown
Chief Creative Officer at Strategies 360

"This is the right time for *The Elephant in the Room*. This book is perfectly positioned to become a catalyst of hard but necessary discussions amongst us. The story draws readers in immediately. Jacobs' direct approach to dealing with social and systemic racial development through the power of parable will have readers questioning their positions while gaining a better understanding of those held by others. This book allows readers to view racial issues from several viewpoints and helps make each one understandable and relatable. I highly recommend this book to all community leaders, business owners, and anyone invested in DEI work for the advancement of our community."

— William F. Collins
author of *Respect the Struggle*

"Reading this book is akin to opening your eyes to every black person's experience. So much so that I had to take deep breaths as I continued to read with intrigue about the experiences Jacobs writes about. Confronting these realities is step one of racial progress. We need more stories like this to show the full experience of brown and Black people in corporate America."

— Cindi Bright
Author of *Color of Courage: Crushing
Racism in Corporate America*

"*The Elephant in the Room* provides readers with a comprehensive journey through the nuances and intricacies that make talking about race difficult for so many of us. Jacobs' use of relatable personas to highlight his observations and techniques in the field of diversity, equity and inclusion is engaging and informative without feeling overtly instructive. Jacobs' effort to tie the chapters of the book together, both in narrative form in Debriefing and in the Afterword, should be appreciated by those working in this field every day. Patrick Lencioni has nothing on Jacobs when it comes to the business parable!"

— Doug Austin
President and CEO of UPD Consulting

"This. is. a. must. read. Period."

— Karen A. Johnson, PhD
Director of Washington State Office of Equity

"*The Elephant in the Room* is a must read for anyone looking to truly understand the psychological warfare that takes place amid racial dynamics in the workplace. This book is uncut, so be prepared! The accuracy of the emotions and clarity of the challenges we face as African Americans in predominately white corporate spaces is unmatched."

— Taliesha Garrett
HR Leader at Boeing

THE
ELEPHANT
IN THE ROOM

A business parable about race and equity
conversations in the workplace

Philip "Sharp Skills" Jacobs

Rebel Firm Books, Tacoma, WA

ISBN 9781736820957

First Edition

Production by Blue Cactus Press

Editing by Kate Threat and Christina Vega

Cover art and design by Knic Pfost

To Phil Jr. and Jonathan. You are my motivation to help make this world a better place.

This book is also dedicated to the people who lost their lives in the Buffalo Massacre, and to their families. Celestine Chaney, Roberta A. Drury, Margus D. Morrison, Andre Mackneil, Katherine Massey, Heyward Patterson, Aaron Salter, Geraldine Talley, Pearl Young, and Ruth Whitfield, may you rest in eternal power.

Contents

This book was not easy to write. Within it, I wanted to convey detailed perspectives on race from people of different racial and ethnic backgrounds. I wrote this book from my own perspective, that of a Black man. A Black man who is also a millenial, cis-gender, straight, able-bodied, politically independent (neither Democrat nor Republican), Christian, entreprenurial, single father from Inglewood, California. I also did research and received input from friends, colleagues, and others whose racial identity is different from mine.

There are bound to be things within these pages that make you uncomfortable, will be disagreeable to you, and might even piss you off. There may be other parts that make you say, "hell yeah!" My goal was to inspire deeper dialogue around the complex topics of race and racial equity dialogue which, hopefully, lends itself to finding solutions to improving the quality of life for Black people, people of color, and ultimately, all people in the United States. Brace yourself, here we go.

– Philip "Sharp Skills" Jacobs

"Many White people may avoid conversations about race out of fear of 'saying the wrong thing.' And many people of color in predominantly White companies may avoid these conversations out of fear of being seen as a complainer — or worse. But pretending the elephant in the room isn't there won't make it go away."

– Dr. Kira Hudson Banks

Derek kept checking his phone as he sat in his pristine Tesla Model S. He turned up the volume a little more to "I Don't Stress" by Nipsey Hussle, a song that motivated him when he was under intense pressure. "*I don't stress out, nigga, poke my chest out, nigga, weight on my shoulder, brings the best out, nigga...*" He was waiting for an email that would decide his fate with his employer, Innovative Energy. Innovative Energy was a tech-based, clean-energy company at which Derek had been promoted to Global Vice President of Talent, Diversity, Equity, and Inclusion eighteen months ago. Derek was appointed to this position by the CEO and Board of Directors to make Innovative Energy a more inclusive environment, especially as it pertained to race. The company had been struggling in this area for several years. Its attrition rates for Black and Latino employees were extremely high, and embarrassing, and as a result the company had a reputation of being racist. Although Innovative Energy was a highly profitable company, the work environment there was affecting its share price, customer sentiments, and brand clout. The company was also losing key talent who were difficult to replace.

When Derek accepted the position at Innovative Energy, he got to work putting out fires and setting up new processes. He started to see tremendous success within a short period of time. In fact, most of the positive press the firm was receiving at the moment was directly tied to Derek's efforts. However, his success and progress rubbed some members of the executive leadership team the wrong way. Derek took his job seriously and would call a spade a spade in meetings. This directly challenged the status quo and privileged mindsets of certain members of the executive leadership team.

While the CEO was in Derek's corner, he was also heavily influenced by Derek's most vocal critics on the executive leadership team. Because of this, the CEO would often say supportive things to Derek in private, but leave him out to dry in leadership team meetings, where it mattered most. Often, Derek, who had been on the executive leadership team the least amount of time compared to other members, was left to fend for himself when pushing his ideas of creating a more inclusive culture within the firm.

The butterflies in Derek's stomach weren't only from the challenges he faced with his employer, though. Derek was also the keynote speaker at the Having the Race Conversation Summit, which would start in less than ninety minutes. Despite how little time he had, Derek couldn't bring himself to get out of his car and walk across the full parking lot to enter the hotel where the summit was being held. At thirty-eight years old, Derek had accomplished more professionally than anyone in his family. But at this moment, he felt a severe case of impostor syndrome. He knew how hard he had worked to get to where he was, but there was always a cloud lingering over his head saying he hadn't done enough. Derek was wise enough to know that what he was experiencing was his own bout of post-traumatic stress disorder, which stemmed from almost two decades of "working while Black" in the White-dominated corporate structures of the United States. He was constantly navigating the pressure to perform without losing himself in the process. The pressure was a side effect of trying to live up to the expectations of White people, many of which included double standards. In recent years, he'd adopted a "fuck it and fuck them if they don't like my Blackness" attitude. Yet, he still couldn't shake the thought that all he had worked for could be snatched away at any given moment, on a whim.

After his third listen to the song, he turned the music off and began to say his morning affirmations, a daily ritual he used to ready himself for the racist corporate behavior he often faced.

"I am enough, I am more than capable, I am valuable. I have the power to create my reality and I choose to be successful in all of my endeavors today."

He stared at himself in his rearview mirror and checked the time on his gold Daytona Rolex. He knew he couldn't stay in his car waiting on that email forever. It was time to get his head in the game.

He took one final, deep breath, opened his car door, stepped out, and walked toward the entrance of the hotel. He walked with all the swagger he could muster. As he stepped through the revolving doors, he took in the magnitude of the moment. It was rare for Derek to feel like his reality matched his sense of self, but this was one of those moments. He looked up at the vaulted ceilings and the exquisite artwork in the foyer, then down at the marble floors. He noticed how the sprawling staircases, covered with deep, maroon-colored carpet with gold accents, led straight to the conference room.

Derek let it all sink in while taking a deep breath. He had stayed at this hotel before, but now that he was the main speaker for the Having the Race Conversation Summit, it felt different. It felt like he had finally made it. Before he could fully enjoy his sense of accomplishment, he was politely but abruptly interrupted by a member of the concierge. She was a White woman who appeared to be in her late twenties.

"Have you been helped, sir"? she asked in a friendly and highly professional tone.

Derek stammered as he came out of his daydream. "Uh, um … no. Well, actually, I'm the keynote for the summit today."

A flash of disbelief crossed her face, which Derek picked up on. She quickly masked it with an affirming smile.

"Indeed, sir. Welcome. Have you been to the Davenport before?"

Derek was a little puzzled by her question. *What did him staying there have to do with him being the keynote speaker for the summit?* He realized he was being a bit defensive. He took a small breath and responded. "Yes, on a few occasions."

"Excellent, if you provide me with your last name and a photo ID, I can look you up in our system before having the event specialist take you where you are supposed to be."

"Absolutely, my last name is Blain."

He took out his black and gray Louis Vuitton wallet to get his license. As he reached for it, he overheard another concierge member about six feet away greeting an older White man who was probably in his late fifties. "Good morning, sir, and welcome," said the young, Asian American male concierge. He couldn't have been older than his mid-twenties.

"Morning! I'm here for the summit," replied the White gentlemen.

"Indeed sir, let me escort you to your destination. Would you care for a cup of our premium coffee?" asked the concierge.

"No, thanks, I just want to get to the summit."

"Indeed sir, right this way." The concierge came out from behind his desk and led the gentleman to the conference room without mentioning ID or asking for a last name.

Derek was stunned. He looked at his concierge, expecting her to say something in response to what he had just witnessed. She didn't appear phased in the slightest. It was as if it hadn't happened. Derek started making mental calculations about what to do. He was trying not to show how pissed off he was. He could make a fuss about this clear display of unequal treatment. Here he was, the keynote of the event, having to provide a name and ID to be let into the summit while a White man who was merely an attendee was given the royal treatment. He was baffled that this could still be taking place in 2023, and at the Having the Race Conversation Summit, of all places. The irony was unbelievable to him. He resolved to put his feelings on ice, keep his composure, and deal with this series of microaggressions *after* the conference. He had been in this emotional territory before and had built up mental resistance that enabled him to operate at a high level, despite unfair treatment. He also reasoned that he may have gotten the concierge member who was a stickler and maybe the whole incident had nothing to do with him being Black. He convinced himself that this was the case. He handed the concierge his driver's license and she proceeded to do some sort of internal check on her computer.

"Everything checks out Mr. Blain. Here's this back," she said in a perky tone, handing him his ID. "If you'll just follow me this way, I'll take you to where you need to be."

She led him down the long hallway toward the escalator. On the way, she said, "I'm so glad they are having this summit, it's so important for our society to become more inclusive of minorities."

Derek nodded in agreement but didn't respond, hoping it would cut the conversation short. He hated being called a minority and he also wasn't feeling this messenger. "You know, my brother's fiancée is Black and I'm really glad she will be a part of our family. She is so sweet," the concierge said with a wide, closed-mouth smile.

By now, Derek was convinced this chick didn't have a clue, but he kept his cool and replied, "is that right?" Internally, he felt for her brother's fiancée. If he was anything like his sister, that fiancée was going to be in for a shitty ride.

"Okay Mr. Blain, this is where we part. It has been a pleasure talking with you. If you head up the escalator, the main conference room will be on your right-hand side. You'll see signs that indicate where you need to go. If you have any trouble, you know where to find me."

The trouble you've given me has prepared for me any other trouble I may come across at this summit, Derek thought to himself. "Thank you," was all he said. He stepped onto the escalator to make his way upstairs.

When Derek got to the third floor, he saw a lively and bustling area full of people of several different racial backgrounds talking and getting ready to step into the main conference room for the summit kickoff. He wanted to get a pulse on the attendees, so he took his time walking up to the registration table. He zeroed-in on two Black women talking to each other by the coffee dispensers.

There was an apparent age gap between them, but their demeanor suggested they were peers.

"Girl, I am not looking forward to this summit. It seems like every White person wants to be my friend afterwards because they had some great awakening. Like, it's good and all that, you finally came to the realization that Black lives matter, but you need to demonstrate that understanding with some real, sustained action before you start trying to get buddy-buddy with me. I've been dealing with racist White folks too long to get excited about them changing as a collective," said the younger woman.

"I agree with you, Keisha, I just hope we can find some common ground at this summit. There is so much racial tension in our world right now, it's at a boiling point and we need more White allies who get it. It's hard, but I'm really trying to put my own cynicism on the back burner to build bridges with White people, or folks of any race for that matter, who want to dismantle racism," replied the older woman.

"I hear you, but I feel like we've seen this story before, and I know how it plays out. A bunch of White folks who think they are woke – I'm so tired of that word by the way – start crusading for Black Lives Matter after one of us gets killed by the police or some 'concerned' White citizen standing their ground. After a month or two, their zeal subsides and we get left picking up the pieces while nothing changes, systemically, that would prevent us from getting killed by law enforcement in the first place. They'll move back into their comfort zones of pushing inclusion that focuses on gender, mainly White women, or the LGBTQ community, or introverts. I'm not saying those aren't important groups to focus on, but I feel like the Black community needs the most attention. We are the ones who are getting killed, the least likely to get promoted to the C-suite, and we still haven't gotten our just due after over 400 years of oppression. I'm tired of getting the short end of the stick, Laura. I don't want to be as cynical as I am, but I'm tired of continuing to be let down. I'm really ready to say 'fuck it,' start my own firm, and leave the good ol' White folks to figure this out for themselves," Keisha said.

They both laughed and kept talking. Derek wanted to keep listening but didn't want to come off as an eavesdropping weirdo. Plus, he really needed to get to the registration table.

As Derek approached the registration table, he checked his phone again to see if he had received the email he was expecting from his CEO. There were only a few emails from his direct reports in his inbox. Derek gave a small sigh of relief but was still on edge in anticipation of the CEO and Board of Directors' decision regarding him. He slipped his phone back into the inner pocket of his black Tom Ford blazer.

Derek was greeted at the speaker registration table by a bronze-skinned, Mexican American woman in her early twenties named Liz. This was her second year at the summit. Last year, she was an attendee. She seemed to be a driven young woman. When she attended the summit last year, she was drawn to the mission, which was "to have effective conversations about race that lead to systemic change." This mission deeply resonated with her, as she was the daughter of immigrants. Before she was born, her mother and father left Mexico to provide their children with an opportunity to get an education good enough to ensure upward mobility. Her father found work as a home construction laborer, which he still did to this day. Her mother found work cleaning homes. Though their jobs are not glamorous, they provided a way for her parents to put two of their children through college. Their third child was just entering their junior year of high school.

"Hi, how are you doing?" the young woman greeted Derek, grinning from ear to ear. "We are excited to hear you speak, Derek. I've watched a bunch of your videos on YouTube and read two of your books. I'm going to buy your third today!"

Derek tried to downplay his positive shock and delight. He was still getting used to the level of success he had attained. "Thank you, I really appreciate your kind words and that you follow my work. But, I'm sorry, I didn't catch your name..." replied Derek. This was the first truly positive exchange Derek had been a part of since he entered the hotel.

"I'm Liz. It's a pleasure to see you again this year. I also hope to be an author and speaker one day. You are truly an inspiration," said Liz.

Still slightly stunned, Derek replied, "Glad to be of service. Let's talk more after the summit about some paths you can take to achieve that."

Liz lit up like a Christmas tree. "Oh my goodness, are you kidding? I would love that!"

Derek couldn't help but notice all the toy elephants on the registration table and in various people's hands in the foyer. "Hey, what are all these?" Derek asked Liz as he picked one up.

Liz smiled. "Well, I'm sure you know that in much of our society and world, race is the elephant in the room. It's something many people don't like to acknowledge. Couple that with race conversations being very stressful, especially when you begin to unpack your own experiences, and things get uncomfortable fast. So, the summit creators had the clever idea of including these stress balls, in the shape of elephants, in every summit welcome packet. They serve as a reminder that we need to address the elephant in the room. And, we can squeeze these little reminders when we find ourselves tensing up about race."

"Wow, that's dope!" beamed Derek.

"Yeah, it is, but if you think that's something, check this out. You can have a sneak peek since you're our keynote." Liz beckoned him to follow her behind the closed conference doors. Derek followed as she cracked the doors wide enough for them to slide into the conference space.

In the conference room, which was the center of the hotel, was a life-sized version of an elephant. It was placed in the middle of hundreds of round tables, placed uncomfortably and almost comically within the middle aisle of 700-plus seats. The elephant was so imposing that Derek didn't hear Liz ask him a question.

"Oh, I'm sorry, what did you say?" he stumbled.

"Have you ever seen anything like it? It's a spectacle, isn't it?" Liz chuckled.

Derek walked up to the elephant statue to get a better look. It wore a big sign around its neck that said "Race." Truly, the organizers of the summit had pulled out all the stops to get their message across.

"It's powerful." Derek said under his breath, staring at the statue.

"Alright, let's head back outside so we can get you checked-in and escorted to the green room." Liz said.

As they were about to head back out through the doors, a hotel staff member stopped them. "You all aren't supposed to be in here yet. Who are you with?"

By this point, Derek had had enough of the prickly staff at the hotel. But before he could give the staff member an earful, Liz responded. "With all due respect, the fact that you would even address us as you have shows me that this establishment has some deeply rooted racist ideologies that still persist to this day. You might see your behavior as you just doing your job, but we see it as microaggressions aimed directly at us. We have our conference badges displayed, which communicates our purpose in this room ahead of the event." Liz stared the staff person down, forcing him to look away.

The staff person looked like a deer caught in headlights. Before he could mumble anything, Liz cut him off. "When you saw a Black man and a Latina woman together, you automatically assumed we didn't belong here and started treating us as if we were trespassing. This is the same mode of thinking that leads to Black people being abused and murdered by police officers at disproportionate rates without any consequence. You didn't inquire about our presence here from a place of helpfulness or service, but from a place of accusation and vitriol. The greatest tragedy of all is you didn't even know you were doing that."

The tension was so thick you could cut it with a knife. The hotel staffer fidgeted, his face turning bright red.

"Well, since accusing minds want to know," said Liz, "Mr. Blain here is the Global head of Talent, Diversity, Equity and Inclusion at Innovative Energy. Maybe you've heard of them? And he is gracing your stage today as the keynote speaker of this summit, which is paying part of your salary. I was giving him a tour of the room for last-minute preparations."

Liz missed her calling, she's definitely more suited to be an attorney, Derek thought to himself. After Liz delivered her speech, she paused, waiting for a response from the befuddled hotel staffer. She knew she was giving him more sassiness than his White privilege could stomach. "I'm just doing my jo – "

Before he could get the full sentence out, Liz fired, "Your *job* is to make sure attendees of this event have a pleasurable experience. Your *job* is to ensure things go as smoothly as possible, not to belittle us with microaggressions stemming from years of racial prejudice and stereotyping. Would you have questioned us the same way if we were White?" Liz paused again, acting as if she was waiting for an answer to her rhetorical question.

Derek, at this point feeling uncomfortable for the staffer and the awkward position he was in after Liz defended him so vigorously, interjected. "Hey, I think we should head back out into the lobby. I still need to get to where I need to be for the event." Derek knew he was falling into one of his bad habits right then, which was connected to a symptom of what Dr. Joy Degruy referred to as "Post Traumatic Slave Syndrome." Post Tramatic Slave Syndrom occurs when Black people try to protect White people from physical and emotional distress, even when they are clearly in the wrong. This had become a regular method Derek employed when things got uncomfortable between him and his White colleagues. He had been doing this since he was a kid, to make and keep friends. As soon as the words came out of his mouth, he knew he was doing it again. Taken aback, Liz responded.

"I guess you're right, let's head back so we don't cause any more mayhem."

Derek could feel her sarcasm. He had clearly sided with the staffer by letting him off the hook, which would give him mental license to carry out the same type of behavior he had just shown Derek and Liz. Derek had also invalidated the highly logical, well-informed, and appropriate response Liz brought forth. He could tell he'd lost some of her respect. When Liz and Derek headed back out into the lobby and the staffer was sure they were out of earshot, he mumbled under his breath, "that's exactly why we are building a wall to keep your asses out."

When they got back to the lobby, Derek could tell Liz was a little dejected from their skirmish with the staffer and Derek's response to it. As if sensing Derek was going to say something about the awkward situation, Liz spoke up first.

"Okay, Mr. Blain, let me hand you over to Stacey. She'll take you to the green room and make sure you are squared away for the rest of your time at the summit." Liz said this without batting an eye. She grabbed her walkie talkie and chirped Stacey, letting her know they were ready for her.

Derek wanted to make things right with Liz. He kept thinking about what he could say to her. He knew he'd hit a deep trigger but he couldn't quite determine what it was, which meant he didn't have an effective way to fix what he'd done. Plus, it seemed as though that ship had sailed. He had deeply disappointed Liz and he knew it. It would be hard to recover from this before the conference started.

At this point, Derek didn't feel up to giving the keynote address. He felt the storm cloud of impostor syndrome hovering within inches of his head. He felt like the chinks in his professional armor were glaringly apparent for everyone to see.

Liz busied herself with other summit attendees as they awaited Stacey. Stacey approached with an infectious smile on her face.

"Hey, Derek!" she announced in her noticeable Southern accent. "It's so nice to meet you."

Before Derek could fully put his hand out to shake hers, Stacey reached out for a hug. "I'm a hugger, bring it on in!" she said, laughing. Derek reached in for a lukewarm embrace, but he was cheered, somewhat, by her jovial spirit. Stacey was a bi-racial woman from Baton Rouge, Louisiana, and was in her early forties. She'd left the South during Hurricane Katrina and was now married with three kids. She'd developed strong acumen in emotional intelligence from being the middle child of seven siblings, as well as from her time as a medic in the Marine Corps. Derek could tell she had a heart of gold, but that she also meant business.

"Mr. Blain, let's get on over to the green room so you can get comfortable," Stacey said with her Southern charm.

Derek, who was relieved to get a moment away from Liz's intense personality, was relieved. "Sounds good. Lead the way."

Derek walked alongside Stacey, who walked somewhat fast, but gracefully. Derek could sense she had dozens of amazing stories she could share. As they walked, he was hoping to find out more about her. She was truly magnetic.

"I am so excited to hear what you have to say, Derek. We are living in such tumultuous times; we need strong Black men who can speak the truth without fear. While there are so many challenges facing us as a nation, the racial awakening that emerged after George Floyd's murder provided a unique window of opportunity for people to come together like they never have before."

Derek couldn't help but say, "umm huh," in agreement.

"You see, I have the benefit of being on both sides. My daddy is White and my momma is Black. This used to be a challenging aspect of my identity to navigate, especially when I was young. When I was in high school, I wasn't White enough to fit-in with the White kids, but I also wasn't Black enough to find community with the Black kids. I was a misfit. For a long time things were difficult for me. That was, until I read the autobiography of Frederick Douglas. When I discovered he was bi-racial like me, it made me proud of my heritage and showed me what was possible. Barack Obama being elected president was another feather in my cap. And when I look at the long list of achievements and contributions of multi-racial people in this country, I have been able to draw strength from that realization. This is a pride and legacy I am doing my best to instill in my children, who are also bi-racial. They don't have as hard of a time fitting in, though, because more of their peers look like them nowadays. The acceptance of bi-racial relationships is so much more prevalent now, too. I think those of us who come from this kind of background are in a unique position to connect with various racial groups, due to our experiences in both realities. But I've been on my soapbox long enough. You are probably ready for me to zip it," Stacey said in a matter-of-fact tone.

"No, please continue. We still have another forty-five minutes before the summit kicks off, right?" Derek was really enjoying Stacey's point of view.

"That's right, we still need to get you to the green room. But we have a few more minutes to kill," replied Stacey.

"Okay, great. You said you never really felt accepted by either the Black or White communities when you were growing up. Why do you think that was? And how did you deal with that?" Derek leaned-in closer, eager for her response.

Stacey thought to herself for a moment, then opened up. "You know, I have my suspicions that the mistreatments I received from both groups were generational in nature, stemming all the way back to when our ancestors were enslaved here in the U.S. and when my ancestors directly enslaved them. As you know, White, male slave owners raped many Black, enslaved women. Those women would then have mixed-race babies who were caught in-between both worlds. Some of these children were treated better by the slave owners because they had lighter skin than other, dark-skinned children. This better treatment was often internalized by the lighter-skinned, enslaved children who got preferential treatment from those who held power. A natural hatred ensued because who doesn't want preferential treatment, right? But to White people, no matter how light skinned those mixed-race babies were, they still weren't White, and therefore had to be rejected. Some of these mixed-race children were even treated worse by slave owners because the wives or family members of the slave owner, usually the head of household, was jealous of the affection he would give to his mixed children.

This is my high-level hypothesis, but I don't think it's too far off the money to assume these sentiments were handed down generationally. My whole life I've had to prove, in some way, how Black I am, and in others, that my White side was more dominant, in order to succeed. But when I hit my late thirties, I got tired of playing both sides. I resolved to be myself. I was emotionally and mentally exhausted because no matter what I did, neither side seemed to accept me. So, I first had to learn how to accept myself. Damn what anybody else thought. I began to see an immediate shift in the quality of my relationships with both groups after I made that decision. Because I started respecting myself, I could resist the urge to pander to either side, which is something I realized I had made a horrible habit of doing all my life. As a result, I began to attract the type of people into my life who loved me for me, regardless of my complexion. Now I have a wonderful mix of people in my circle from several racial backgrounds, including Black and White. This isn't to say life is always peachy. There are still a lot of people out there who say a lot of stupid shit, like 'What are you?' or 'Can I touch your hair?' I've gotten really good at verbally popping these people upside the head in a diplomatic manner. It's a skill I developed with a lot of practice and a few gray hairs."

They busted out laughing. Derek said, "yeah, I feel you. I remember, around the time President Obama got elected to his first term, so many White and Asian people told me I reminded them of him. Sometimes when I walked into stores in Koreatown, the first thing they would say to me was, 'Obama.' At first, it was deeply offensive because I knew they were lumping all Black men together based on one they were knowledgeable about, rather than treating me as an individual. Don't get me wrong, Obama is a great person to be compared to, and it's better to be stereotyped as him than as a criminal or thug, which Black men are often labeled as. But at the same time, it's incredibly lazy and dangerous to assume we are all the same."

"So how did you deal with these types of situations?" Stacey asked. She was hoping to share some of Derek's tips with her oldest son, who was about to be a high school freshman.

Derek responded matter-of-factly. "For one, I've had to learn to choose my battles wisely. Not every racial offense deserves a response. I learned I only have so much energy to give and it's valuable. I need to be strategic with where I place it. I don't always get it right, but I try to gauge the impact a conversation will have on someone's enlightenment after they have said something offensive. If I feel a particular person's well-intentioned, I may decide to educate them on the error of their words and how they can do better in the future. I know that puts me in the often-stigmatized *race teacher* category, but I'm willing to be that in the moment if I feel it will lead to helping a person change.

Over time, I've developed a running list of crafting pre-scripted responses to ignorant comments. I've found that often, when people say something racially offensive, they don't even know it. A comment like, 'that's interesting, I'd like to hear more about how you came to that conclusion about me,' jars them, catches them off guard, and forces them to think about what they just said. When I've said this to people who exhibit extreme racial bias, they often apologize and it invites a constructive conversation. It also puts me in the position of correcting their erroneous point of view without coming off like *the angry Black man* in the process. Much the same way as you, this knowledge was earned with some gray hair. This is why it's important to pass information to our kids about how to navigate racialized terrain effectively. We need to prepare them and give them confidence to nip microaggressions in the bud."

"I heard that!" Stacey responded. "It really does take time to get good at addressing these things. I mean, just because we have so much lived experience around racial dynamics doesn't mean we have it all figured out. Speaking for myself, I know I can assume things about people from other racial groups. I'm guilty of making fun of some of the common characteristics some groups exhibit. I'm also learning how to see people who are different from me as individuals, as opposed to placing them all in the same category. It's not always easy, especially with White people. They have been the source of so much of my pain. But I have some White folks in my life who have also been some of my greatest allies."

"Same here," Derek affirmed. "At the end of the day, we are all trying to live our best lives, be successful, and take care of our families. And we are having to do it in front of a horrific historic backdrop that still haunts us to this day. It's painful. Black and White people both must come to grips with how ugly the racial experience has been for Black, Latino, Asian, Pacific Islander, Indigenous, and bi-racial people here. It's hard to reveal the baggage we carry, especially when there's no guarantee the person we are revealing it to will accept it as truth. Still, we have to try." said Derek.

"Exactly, we gotta keep climbing and becoming the change we want to see." replied Stacy. "Well, I think we've killed a significant amount of time, but we'll have to continue this conversation later. Let's get you settled in the green room. Your assistant told us you are a tea aficionado, so there is something waiting inside for you that I think will make you smile."

"You don't ever have to threaten me with tea surprises," said Derek. They both laughed as Derek followed behind Stacey and they entered the green room. As they walked in, Derek took a quick glance at the email app on his phone to see if anything had come from Innovative Energy. The board's decision was still weighing heavily on his mind.

THE GREEN ROOM

Derek and Stacey entered a beautifully laid out green room. Inside, a buffet waited for them, filled with more food than any of the ten speakers and presenters could hope to eat. There were two flat screen TV's on both sides of the room broadcasting the news. There were even massage chairs with headphones connected to them to allow users to hear sounds of nature and serenity while they sat down. Peanut butter brown leather sofas, love seats, and oversized chairs dotted the space. Had Derek not just experienced microaggressions, he would have been able to enjoy himself.

"Ok, Mr. Blain, this is where you will be until it's time for you to speak. You'll be able to watch the summit here, if you'd like. We should have all of the food and beverages you need for a comfortable experience. If there is anything else you need, don't hesitate to let any of the conference staff know. I'll be back and forth between the conference room and here to check on you and make sure you're informed of the schedule. Please get acquainted with the other conference speakers," Stacey said.

Derek was hoping he could sneak into some of the sessions to be around people who would be truly experiencing the event. But he was still polite. "You got it, thanks so much for all your help and for the great conversation."

"My absolute pleasure, Mr. Blain," said Stacey.

"Please call me Derek, no need to be so formal."

"Oh I just can't help it, it's the Baton Rouge in me," Stacey said with a soft chuckle as she exited the room.

Derek looked around, then headed straight for the food. He wasn't one to pass up a quality buffet. He noticed the diverse racial backgrounds of the other facilitators. There was an older White man, probably in his mid-sixties, sitting at the corner table, speaking with an Indian woman who looked to be around forty years old. At the far end of the room, an Asian man in his thirties was listening intently to a senior Black man. Derek couldn't quite hear what they were talking about, but it appeared to be a deep conversation. There was also an Indigenous woman, probably no older than thirty, chatting with a White woman in her mid-to-late thirties at the bar, within earshot. Everyone seemed to be having such meaningful conversations that the only person who acknowledged Derek was the older back man. The old man gave Derek a signal, a casual salute.

Derek wanted to feel out the vibe of the room before he introduced himself to anyone, and he was hungry, so he decided to eat first and then pick his moment to mingle. After he fixed his plate and sat down, the White woman approached him.

"Hi, I'm Alex. You must be Derek."

Derek was a little annoyed. She was disrupting the strategy he had just worked out in his head. But he managed to eke out a smile. "That's correct, nice to meet you, Alex."

"I've heard a lot of amazing things about you. Do you mind if I join you?"

"Not at all." Derek lied.

Alex sat across from him and smiled, completely unaware. "You know, this is really awesome, all of us coming together..." Alex said.

"Yes, it is." Derek started nibbling on a mini barbeque wing. He knew he wouldn't be able to enjoy it the way he wanted to while talking to her. He was sensitive about the stereotype that Black people love to eat chicken. While this was true for him, he hated leaning into any social stigma the media placed on Black people at their expense. He felt somewhat forced to interact with her, either way.

"Now is the time for us to not only have these conversations about racism and White privilege, but come up with real solutions that will allow us to move forward together," Alex continued.

Derek just nodded his head, not really knowing how to respond. He wasn't sure if she was being genuine or only trying to earn cool points for sounding *woke*. He gave her the benefit of the doubt. She had to have some higher level of perspective on these things to be in *this* room for *this* summit, right? Still, he thought it was odd for her to launch into a conversation about these topics after just meeting him. It caught him off guard. But he kept listening to be polite, as well as to see if and when she was going to put her foot in her mouth.

"I'm so glad I get to be included in this work with all of you," she said. "Sometimes, this fight for greater equity can be lonely, especially when you look like me. I've lost friends and family over my beliefs about Black Lives Matter and the systemic oppression of people of color."

Derek, sensing this conversation was about to go in a direction he didn't want it to, tried to lighten the mood before it fully settled. "Yeah, DEI has to be one of the worst strategies to win friends and influence people."

"Tell me about it, I've gotten into three-hour debates over Thanksgiving dinner with relatives who voted for our current president. They just don't see how divisive and racist he is, and it's hard to tolerate them," Alex affirmed.

Derek resisted the knee-jerk reaction to agree with her. He had learned that sometimes, White people say things like this to prove how *woke* they are in the DEI space without having paid the price to earn it. He wanted to believe Alex was genuine, especially because she was a facilitator. But he had seen too many people of various racial backgrounds seeking to profit from DEI work instead of actually changing things. He didn't feel there was anything wrong with being well-compensated for one's work in inclusion and diversity, but that compensation needed to be earned by those whose work comes from a genuine place.

Derek kept eating his food and didn't respond, though he kept eye contact with Alex. At this point, the conversation was awkward for both of them. Alex's intuition told her she may have come on a little strong and hadn't yet earned the right to dive deep into a conversation about race with Derek yet. Trust hadn't been established. She shifted gears. She genuinely wanted to talk to him. "So, is this your first year at the summit?"

Derek was relieved. "Yes, and it's been ... an experience so far." He had been dealing with a lot of bullshit at the summit already but didn't want to say that outright. Again, he didn't know if Alex was trustworthy enough for him to open up to her.

Alex pressed, "It can be intense right? Tell me more."

Derek was starting to get a little irritated, but he stayed cordial. "You know, I just feel tension in the air. Maybe it's just me, but it feels like even at a summit such as this, there is still a lot of work to do in facilitating how people relate to each other across racial differences. The spotlight is on that topic here, so it feels glaringly apparent when someone isn't good at it."

"In those instances, isn't it important to factor in someone's intentions? At least they're trying, right? They could just go on about their lives without engaging in these conversations. People have to be given room to grow and learn so they can get better at building relationships across racial differences."

Derek sensed Alex had taken what he'd said personally. He wasn't going to save her from her feelings, though. It wasn't his responsibility. He knew that if she continued to wrestle with these questions, it could lead to her growth and development. "It sounds like you have some unique views on intent versus impact as it pertains to conversations on race. Tell me more about the people who are trying to get it right but could go on with their lives without engaging in these conversations if they chose to."

Alex realized she didn't have a good answer, but she attempted to save face. "I personally feel everyone has a responsibility to engage in conversations about race, even people who think they don't need to. Our country can never truly heal if we don't, and that will stall the great gains we have made in this area."

Derek almost laughed in her face. Instead, he composed himself, knowing he was in a pivotal moment in their conversation that could either lead to growth or a shut down. He didn't know Alex well, but he knew she could become an effective ally if she was given room to grow into one. He also didn't take it for granted that she was in the green room with him. She must be doing *something* right in her area of expertise concerning racial inclusion.

All of this ran through Derek's mind in milliseconds. After a brief pause, he decided to overcome his cynicism, though justified, and build a bridge instead. "I absolutely agree. Tell me more about your work and the ways you are pushing this agenda forward."

Alex beamed from ear to ear, feeling the new connection they had made. She leaned forward and began to explain all she was up to in her work as an advocate of racial equity.

Across the room, the older White man was listening intently to the Indian woman's story.

"When I told him I refused to keep being stepped over, I knew I had to come up with a plan to be independent," said Fatima. "Indian men often take a dominant role over their wives. The culture is beginning to change, slowly, for those of us in America, though. More Indian women are staking their claim and finding their own voices. But there is still a traditional mindset that keeps many of us from taking risks to be our own person. But I have this fire in my belly that won't let me be someone else's possession.

In many ways, I feel like I am an outsider because I don't play by the rules my culture has laid out for me. Even though the caste systems in India were banned several decades ago, they are still very much a part of how we relate to each other socially. My caste, the Dalit, is at the lowest level of the system and is treated the worst. To those born in the U.S., that doesn't mean much. But when I see another Indian person, it's the first thing that comes to mind. It's similar to how Blacks and Whites stereotype each other when they first meet. It is a big part of how we have been conditioned.

When I made the choice to become a software engineer, I knew that career choice would bring more friction into my home because I would earn more money than my husband, who is from the Shudras caste. We already had big problems within our family because we secretly married. Inter-caste marriages are violently resisted in India.

Add to that a Dalit woman earning more than a Shudra man and we had big problems, which we are still working through now.

But, I did it anyway and I'm so glad I did. Now, I'm not just tolerated in my home, but respected as an equal. And luckily, I married a good man who is willing to grow. Now many of my friends, who are also Indian women, are wanting to step out and have careers of their own."

"That is an incredible story, Fatima," Kevin said. "It sounds like you are continuing to be successful despite the cultural headwinds you have faced, even up to the present moment. How did you end up in racial equity work, and how does your career as a software engineer intersect?"

"You ask such good questions! Honestly, I stumbled into racial equity work. As you probably know, the tech field is very White and Indian-male dominated. Often, I have found myself as the only Indian woman in the room. And sometimes, Indian men can be just as condescending as White guys. Because of that, I haven't been able to find a substantive community after nine years of being in this work.

So, I started speaking out, again. I could not accept the status quo. People on my team and business unit began to take notice of my passion. Other people of color who were marginalized began to come forward and speak up because of *my* boldness. We made such a ruckus that the CEO decided to hold a town hall for our business unit. We were given a forum to air our grievances and also highlight solutions. Our solutions included evaluating our recruitment pool to determine where we were missing the mark as it pertains to having a pipeline of racially diverse talent. We also advised that incentives and bonuses be tied to inclusion and diversity targets being met, with a specific focus on race. Up until that point, our organization was sixty percent White men and women, and thirty-seven percent Indian men.

I'll be honest, I lost quite a few friends over how hard I was pushing for racial equity, especially because to some degree, I was benefitting from being Indian. But I couldn't unsee the bias and discrimination that was highly accepted, even encouraged, in my business unit. Plus, I already felt like an outsider, so it wasn't difficult for me to get over losing friends who wanted to keep business as usual with racial exclusion.

Long story short, we were granted a budget and some authority from the CEO to start a task force for racial equity work. This new role became so time-consuming I had to split my time between being an engineer and a DEI practitioner. We had so much success in the area of racial inclusion that our task force was made an official strategic department and I moved into racially focused DEI work full-time."

"That's incredible! What significant strides do you feel have been made as a result of your work?" Kevin asked.

"For starters, we saw dramatic improvement in accountability of how those in majority racial groups speak to those in minority groups. When I first started at the organization, I would often hear and be the recipient of off-hand jokes related directly to my racial background. And, on several occasions, I witnessed other people of color be humiliated and bear the brunt of microaggressions. The environment was toxic. It reminded me of how the caste system functions in India. I could not stand by and allow it. It was personal for me.

So, one of the first things the task force did was create forums for people to share their experiences in the workplace, good and bad. We highlighted the voices of those who were often overlooked and unheard. The forums also acted as a data gathering tool so we could organize concerns into areas of focus. We turned these focus areas into reports that we brought to the attention of upper level leadership as often as we could.

We did face backlash, and some managers did retaliate, but we stayed committed to the process. I think that was the key. Our task force was unwavering in pushing our agenda and we supported each other. After we caused enough ruckus, other people who were not a part of the task force were emboldened to share their stories and how they had been affected by our work culture.

At that point, legal got involved. And slowly but surely, we saw leadership get serious about changing the culture to become more racially inclusive. Some of the more bigoted members of the leadership team resigned when they saw the culture would not tolerate their behavior any longer. The leadership team realized the company would be in jeopardy if word about the workplace culture went public. I mean, there were unfathomable things going on that the company could have easily been sued over. But, we have some wise people on our task force who know that diversifying our ranks meant nothing if we didn't work on weeding out the bias in the organization and creating a racially inclusive environment first. If we didn't do the hard work of changing our culture first, people of color who joined the organization would exit as soon as they came in.

One of the hardest battles we fought with the leadership team was convincing them that pumping-up recruiting efforts for people of color was not enough. They wanted to create these elaborate recruitment strategies and roll them out to the press to make it appear as if we were a racially inclusive company. Leadership set hiring goals for Black and Latino talent, specifically. We resisted this approach because it was like utilizing a band aid for a gunshot wound. We needed a massive overhaul of the collective paradigm in order for diverse hiring to have any long term effect. Essentially, if leadership had carried out their plans to focus only on recruiting people of color and not working on workplace culture, they would have tokenized all the new hires. I lost sleep over this. The task force's agenda, at that point, was to develop a system of accountability that would require the key culture influencers at the company to earn their way into being called 'racially inclusive leaders.'"

Kevin interjected. "You mentioned you and some of your colleagues faced backlash from some of the managers because of your efforts. How were you able to weather that storm? How did you all support each other?"

"The retaliations were subtle at first. Some of us reported not receiving information that was important to our work. Sometimes this meant we weren't included in meetings or team huddles that we had an absolute right to be at. Things like this come off as an oversight at first, but then patterns emerged. It's an energy you feel, you know, when people are talking *about* you and not *with* you... Then, some of us on the task force were passed over for promotions and projects we were already slated for. Working relationships that were once pleasant turned cold and distant. Some of my colleagues became very stressed and others got physically sick due to the pressure of the environment.

But the positive in all of this is that these struggles made us closer. We were like war buddies passing around our battle stories. Many of us had been working for this company for five years or more, so we were invested in changing its trajectory, and we knew the culture well. We had all built support networks during our tenure there. We were able to lean on these networks at some of our lowest points. I personally had a colleague, a White woman, who was and still is a sounding board. She was a key ally to me. Her support helped balance the anger I felt toward White people who tried to harm me professionally. Our dynamic helped me not view all White people and relationships with them as the same.

Another thing the task force did was prioritize meeting at least once a week to report not only on our progress, but also how we were coping with the oppositions we came against. It was, and still is, critical for us to be honest about how we're feeling and to regularly measure our sentiment over time. Doing the work of racial inclusion is hard enough, especially when the people who you report to are deliberately trying to sabotage you.

A huge win for us, though, was when the CEO and a handful of members on the leadership team acknowledged the importance of racial equity at the enterprise level. This happened after the murder of George Floyd. Their sponsorship acted as a shield in many ways, and gave us cover as we battled with the status quo."

Kevin chimed in. "The truth is, if a company really wants to become racially inclusive, they will invest in it. And they will stay committed over a long period of time. These types of organizational changes often don't bear significant fruit until year five."

"So true! This is my fourth year in this role and we are barely scratching the surface. Unfortunately, there still isn't a Black person on the leadership team, despite the progress we've made. While the CEO has thrown money at the issue, I haven't seen significant movement in diversifying the ranks, nor a true commitment to the work that would make this possible. Leadership has put most of their focus and budget on cultural awareness and anti-bias training. And while these are important first steps, they are not enough on their own."

"Totally agree, there has to be a change of heart that causes the leadership team to seek-out how to solve systemic issues in the organization. Racial bias that is not spoken about will still hide in the shadows. Silence from leadership gives permission for racial inequity to continue to exist. And it takes radical leadership to buck against this silence."

"Well said. Please tell me more about yourself, Kevin. I feel like we've only been talking about me this whole time!"

"You're much more interesting!" Kevin laughed. "Where do I start?" He sighed before continuing. "Long story short, I'm a former politician who quit politics because I was tired of the bullshit. I'm somewhat of an odd fellow among my peers because I actually give a damn about dismantling White supremacy.

I grew up in a predominantly White neighborhood, went to predominantly White schools and most of my experiences when I was younger centered on my Whiteness. But something irked me to my core when I saw people mistreated, especially if they were people of color. So, I decided to do something about it and I thought politics was the way to do it. I'll admit, I did have a White savior complex, but didn't know it at the time.

I started the way most aspiring politicians do out here: I ran for city councilman. From there, I ran for mayor, then congressman. And you know what? I discovered during my ascension up the political ladder that it is rare to find politicians who put the wellbeing of the people who helped them into office over their personal wellbeing. I'm ashamed to say that for probably half of my career, I was one of these people and didn't know it. I mistook taking photo-ops with Black people in my district as actually doing the work necessary to help eradicate the oppression they were living under. My life in office became more about fundraising, securing a loyal voter base, and making guest appearances than about creating change for my constituents. I became like innumerable other public officials I loathed when I was growing up, who said the right things to get the vote but did nothing when they got into office.

I saw Black men and women brutalized and killed by bad cops in my district and I did nothing about it. When it came time to address the media, I gave well-prepared speeches that made people think I was more effective than I was at correcting these issues.

My hypocrisy began weighing on me. I developed a secret alcohol addiction. This almost cost me my marriage. On the outside, I was living the American dream. I had status, power, money, a traditional family, and an expensive home, but I was full of inner turmoil. I was spiraling down. Reality hit home for me one night as I was leaving my office. I saw a colleague of mine, an older White guy like me, sexually harassing his assistant. His assistant at the time was a younger Black woman. He didn't hear or see me, but I heard him in his office telling her that he could change her life because of the influence he had. He said he had made political stars out of other women similar to her. He literally said, 'all you have to do is let me have my way with you tonight. I'll be a good 'massa' to you.' His assistant smacked him before he could blink an eye and stormed out his office. Rightfully so. She wielded more courage in that slap than I had in my fifteen-year-career in public office. My colleague, let's call him jerkface, yelled some of the most gut-wrenching racial slurs I had ever heard in my life at that moment. You would've thought we were living in the Antebellum South.

By this time, I needed to make my presence known, so I casually walked by his office. His assistant – former assistant that is – was long gone. I said to him, 'hey jerkface, everything alright?' He was clearly flustered that he hadn't gotten his way, as he was used to, and his ego was reeling from the young woman's response. But he looked me in the eye and replied, 'All good, Kevin, everything is all good here, buddy,' as if what had just happened hadn't. I was at a total loss. And this was another senior public official, mind you. He was someone I deemed honorable up until that day.

It was then that the veil was lifted for me. I began to reevaluate everything around me. How was it that we, Americans, were so far removed from the transatlantic slave trade, peonage, the Black codes, and the Jim Crow Era, yet a public official in a city as seemingly progressive as ours could treat a Black woman like that? I knew my conscience wouldn't survive if I didn't begin to use my influence the right way.

So, for the rest of my term, I got serious about creating and pushing legislation that would benefit Black people and other people of color who were often marginalized. I spent a lot less time on the golf course, country club, and at dinner parties, and got to work for the people in my district, instead.

My colleagues couldn't accept the new leaf I had turned. People I once considered friends turned into enemies, fast. I always knew politics was a dirty game, but now I was on the receiving end of it. My once highly esteemed colleagues did everything in their power to sabotage and subvert every bill I put forth. I became an outcast and my political clout was no more.

At first, I felt sorry for myself. It's hard to go from being popular to being someone no one wants to eat lunch with. My stances on issues were too controversial and disruptive to the White establishment, the establishment I enjoyed and benefited from. In many ways, I still benefit from this establishment, because of my Whiteness, but now it's harder for me to accept.

So after my term, I quit. I started writing books and speaking about racial inclusion and equity. I've done a few consulting gigs here and there for companies, and somehow, I ended up here."

"Thank you for sharing that. You could have easily accepted your favorable position in life and remained quiet about the overt and covert inequity happening around you. But you decided to become a real ally. One thing I'm curious about is what legislation got so much blowback?"

"When the numbers of Black and Brown people being brutalized by bad cops began to swell, I tried to push a police reform bill. I wanted to see new methods of accountability and oversight for how our law enforcement carried out their duties when it came to people of color, mainly Black and Latino. Within that bill, there were requirements to move some of the funding for police departments toward education, social services, and health care programs. Those who opposed me said I was trying to shut down the police using the triggering language of 'defunding.' The interesting thing, though, is that police budgets have risen over the last forty years, while other much needed services, such as mental health and community development, which by the way are more effective at reducing crime, have decreased. I saw a huge disconnect between how law enforcement agencies were spending their money and what citizens really needed. I felt a new community center would do a better job at crime reduction than providing small tanks and military-grade rifles to local officers. This bill would also have reallocated some police spending toward including mandatory training for non-lethal de-escalation methods, which could potentially lead to less deaths by cops.

Another measure within that bill would have required new police officers joining the force to live within a five-mile radius of the communities they served. To me, that just makes sense. You are more likely to treat people with a deeper sense of dignity, respect, and empathy when you are neighbors with them. We did a study and found that most of the police officers who brutalized people in my district lived an average of twenty miles away from the areas they patrolled. This means those officers had no vested interest in the community they served and the impact their overly aggressive actions might have on the residents. There was even a provision in the bill to provide moving incentives to current officers who wanted to move closer to their beat.

The most controversial section of the bill, though, was to hold police officers and their precincts financially responsible when they injured or killed someone. One sneaky little secret of city and state governments is that taxpayers are the ones who have to foot the bill when families file wrongful death suits. But going after a police officer's pension and a department's budget could lead to more officers using their better judgment when engaging people of color.

When I started to push this bill through, I received death threats and was told my political career would be over if it passed."

"Wow, that's terrible. It's a human tragedy when people get punished for trying to help others."

"That's the world of politics. And it's precisely the reason I got out. I saw that most of my colleagues were all about serving their own interests above those they are supposed to represent. That's not to say there aren't some politicians who are really trying to make a difference in congress, but there aren't enough. And the ones who do want to change things face a major uphill battle from the status quo. The government has the power to heal a lot of our social issues, but they often don't want to use resources toward that. Then, when a Black man gets killed by trigger-happy police, politicians want to hold press conferences and send condolences to the families and talk about how things will be different next time, without ever addressing the underlying issue."

"Ain't that the truth." said James, the older Black man, as he walked past Fatima and Kevin. He didn't miss a beat. "That type of regular inaction sends a clear message that our loved ones don't matter to the highest level of government officials. This same sentiment trickles down to the rest of society. Sorry y'all, I didn't mean to hijack your conversation. That last statement you made hit home for me," James said.

"No problem at all, I'd love to hear more of your perspective," said Kevin.

"Thanks, maybe a little later. I just came over to get a bottle of water. Zhang Wei and I are in a pretty deep discussion of our own," James tapped the couch twice. He turned to head back to where he had been sitting.

"Most definitely, I'm going to hold you to that, good sir."

James sat down with two bottles of water in hand. Zhang sat quietly, trying to hold back his tears. He was usually good at hiding how he was truly feeling, even to himself. But James had managed to pull something out of him that he had kept buried for over five years. "Thanks for the water," Zhang said in a melancholic tone. "I just don't usually talk about this, so it got to me. But I'll be alright."

James nodded his head in agreement. As a DEI veteran, he knew it was important to let Zhang have his moment without someone rushing in to fix things. Zhang hadn't given himself space to process the death of his wife, which is what they'd been discussing. She'd committed suicide a few years back. Zhang, head down, took a sip of his water and chuckled.

James had to know what Zhang found so amusing. "What is it, man?"

"In the last thirty minutes, I've shared things I haven't told anyone, even in my own community, to a big Black man I hardly know." Zhang looked down at his hands. "Please don't be offended. It's just ironic. I'm ashamed to say I haven't been exposed to a lot of positive Black men, other than Obama. Most of what I know has come from the media and hip-hop music. When you're Chinese

American, it's sort of easy to stay within your own bubble, especially when you are well-to-do financially."

"I appreciate your honesty," said James. "But as much as I love hip-hop, especially what it stood for in its inception, it has been used as a tool by the media and greedy record label execs to spread a lot of misinformation. That aside, I'm honored you felt like you could open up to me about what happened to your wife. I can't begin to imagine how painful that was, or still is," James said. He hoped he wasn't showing the twinge of offense he'd felt from Zhang's comments. He was doing his best to make this moment about Zhang.

"In that case, I guess the media has done a number on both of our communities, albeit with different outcomes," Zhang chimed in. "Much like Black Americans, Chinese Americans have fought hard for acceptance here. Once we started gaining some traction, collectively, the model minority myth really did a number on us. I mainly blame my wife's suicide on the pressure she felt to live-up to this myth. The pressure to perform and be above reproach just isn't sustainable. It's something that has caused many Chinese Americans, especially women, to have higher rates of suicide than any other racial group in the U.S. But we've been conditioned over generations to not talk about it, to just put our heads down and excel." Zhang started to tear up again.

James reached over and put a hand on his shoulder to offer some comfort. The moment was clunky, emotional, and beautiful at the same time. The others in the room started to take notice but tried to act as if they weren't listening.

Zhang continued. "In some respects, society does not allow us to access our full humanity. And many of us are taught to not buck against the system. Yet, it's this very system that is causing us so much pain. And it has created division between us and the Black and Latino communities. I believe that term, model minority, was meant to be a direct insult to other minority groups, especially those who have endured centuries of exclusion based on their skin color."

"I remember when that article in *Time Magazine,* 'Those Asian American Whiz Kids', which came out in like, '86 or '87, first introduced that term. Unfortunately, I bought into the stereotype. The Asian kids I went to school with were perceived as the smartest and hardest-working students. Years later, I learned how damaging this myth was to your community," James said.

"I can't speak for all Asians, of course, because our experiences are so different. But we often get lumped together, which leads to more frustration when the model minority myth comes into play. I'm what you call the 'Westernized image' of the stereotypical Asian American. But Asian people come in a wide variety… Japanese, Korean, Filipino, and Vietnamese. There are also those who identify as Black-Asian; their narrative hardly ever gets acknowledged. But yes, that myth has wreaked a lot of havoc on the Chinese American community and other ethnic groups of Asian descent. The Western view of the world can be so ignorant at times. People forget how large Asia is and the wide array of countries that are a part of the continent. I mean, technically, Russians, Afghans, Israelis, and Turks can all be considered Asian."

"I never thought about it like that, but you're right," said James. "It's easy to forget how big and diverse the world is when you're conditioned to see things a certain way. Now correct me if I'm wrong, but I think I read somewhere that the term 'Asian American' was coined during the Civil Rights Era as a way of solidifying the voice and power of those of Asian descent in the U.S., and who were fighting for equality here. I just want to make sure I'm understanding that part of history correctly, 'cause I'll be honest with you, Zhang, I find myself using 'Asian American' quite a bit and want to make sure I'm not causing pain in the process."

"I appreciate you checking. Most people don't. Yes, you are right that mostly Chinese, Japanese, and Korean people who had made their home in the U.S. unified and pushed for our equality. Back then, each group comprised such a small percentage of the overall population that it was important for us to combine forces to amplify our message. I prefer to be called Chinese American. As I said, there are so many groups who can fit into the Asian or Asian American labels that I feel it's important to be specific. You know, since you brought it up, I've always wondered if 'Black American' or 'African American' is the preferred choice for your community?"

James laughed. They were getting comfortable with each other. "It really depends. Some of us prefer Black Americans because it speaks to the culture we have developed in the U.S., despite all the obstacles we've had to overcome and are still overcoming. Others prefer African American because they want to identify with our ancestral homeland, where our ancestors were stolen from. Personally, some days I like Black American and others, African American. Hell, somedays, I just prefer to be called Black. As much as I love this country, I'm not always proud to have 'American' in my identity descriptor because even to this day, we are treated as outsiders. It's difficult to accept this when you practice inclusion for a living. We're trained to recognize bias in its various forms, so I can't unsee it even when I want to."

"I guess that's when the saying, ignorance is bliss, is most applicable, eh?"

James paused for a moment. "Well sort of, but even if a Black person is ignorant of the systemic racism in the U.S., in most cases, they are still impacted by it. Perhaps they see it as something else and it impacts them differently. But that pain is there, nonetheless."

"I see similarities in our communities when it comes to this," said Zhang. "Many of us put our heads down and work in order to ignore the exclusion that has become part of our experience. I personally feel that things are going well, overall, for our community. I know some would disagree, but I've been able to gain access to opportunities in the U.S. that could only be dreamed of in China. Model minority myth aside, I believe if you work hard in this country, you can be successful."

"Well, cheers to that. And on that note, I need to hit the men's room. I've been holding it in for a hot minute."

"Ok sure, but what is a hot minute?" Zhang asked.

James got up and stretched. "It's just slang for 'a long time.'"

"Ah, gotcha... hot minute..." Zhang said to himself, trying to store the term in his mind. On his way out, he noticed Sayen, an Indigenous woman, leaning against the wall in the corner, by herself. She was scrolling through her phone. "Hey Sayen, you doing alright?" James asked, not trying to show his full concern.

"I'm good James, thanks," Sayen said in her always-confident and warm tone. James gave her the thumbs up and headed into the hallway.

Sayen scanned the breakout room sessions on her phone.

Breakout 1: Do Black Lives Matter to Y'all Yet?
Breakout 2: Exploring Today's Indigenous Narrative.
Breakout 3: White People Are Diverse, Too.
Breakout 4: The DEI Revolution or the Status Quo in Disguise?
Breakout 5: My Country 'Tis of Thee, Sweet Land of Misery.
Breakout 6: Getting Comfortable with the "R" Word, Reparations.

THE KICK-OFF

Hello again, everyone. May I please have your attention for just one moment?" Stacey announced after she slipped into the room. "The summit is going to start in exactly ten minutes." She waited for the room to settle before continuing. "Please direct your attention to the monitor just ahead of you. You all will be able to watch the kickoff with Pamela Harris, the summit founder on this screen. After the ice breaker and opening exercises, Pamela will ask participants to head to their breakout sessions. Those of you leading sessions should head to your rooms at 8:50 AM so you can set up. Are there any questions?" Stacey paused for a moment as folks shook their heads to say no.

Zhang spoke up. "What if someone says something really offensive? How should we handle that?"

It was an honest question, but everyone looked away from Zhang and at each other, puzzled. Immediately, Zhang felt he'd lost credibility with the group. Before anyone could respond, Zhang tried to clean it up. "I ask because sometimes, it's good to know how other people are handling conflict, so we can come to an agreement of common methodology. It can be especially helpful for facilitators during the event," Zhang concluded.

Sensing his discomfort, Fatima interjected. "That's a great point Zhang. We have so many skilled facilitators and communicators here. It would be great to hear some tips on what to do if tensions escalate."

Zhang was relieved Fatima affirmed his question.

Sayen perked up. She was trained in conflict management. When she spoke, everyone waited in anticipation. "We all know talking about race in a public setting like this can potentially detonate landmines. A few methods I've used throughout my career, which have served me well, are not responding defensively and staying in control of the situation."

"Ooh, say more," Alex leaned in toward Sayen.

"As a Native woman, I've heard some of the most obtuse and racist things come out of peoples mouths." Sayen adjusted her posture, noticing she had everyone's rapt attention. "I've had to learn how not to outright shut them down or go tit-for-tat. That behavior doesn't build bridges. It causes people to dig their heels deeper into their bias.

I've also learned it's important to know what triggers *me* when talking about race and be truthful about that with people upfront. Unexpectedly, that built my credibility with clients. Although I'm a DEI professional, I'm a human first, and people need to understand that. There are some who don't know enough about the oppression of Natives to care deeply about it, which is often why they say and do stupid things to my people. By managing my defensiveness, I can stay in the conversation and inform them of the Native experience in the context of my own story, and the stories of others I know. This leads to my ultimate goal of building bridges of understanding and mutual respect.

My intentionality around not getting defensive and staying open and reflective, instead, allows me to stay in control of the situation. People tend to want to run away or wall-up when they are confronted with conflict within their conversations, especially when that conflict is related to race. But running away is one of the worst ways to react, especially as a facilitator. When I stay engaged and in control of the situation, I'm focusing on directing the dialogue, not the *content*. I learned this from Derald Wing Sue. It takes courage for people to express strong emotions when talking about race. Doing so can lead to productive outcomes. When touchy topics, like racism, come up in conversation, people deflect and try to go in a different direction to alleviate their discomfort. This either produces conflict and stunts growth that could take place if they'd stayed on topic.

A lot of facilitators will buckle under this pressure and succumb to the loudest voices in the room, losing control of both the content and the process of the dialogue. But I like to let the difficult conversation continue. I focus on the *quality* of the conversation. By acknowledging the feelings of those in disagreement, we can then uncover why people feel the way they do, which gives us something to work with as we, again, seek to build bridges of understanding and respect," Sayen finished.

"That's a mic drop!" Derek said from across the room. Everyone laughed.

"Thank you for sharing your wisdom, Sayen," said Stacey. She waited a moment before continuing. "I also want to direct everyone's attention to the 'RIGHTS' Conversation Approach that Pamela

Harris developed, which can be found on the summit homepage and notebook. This approach ties directly into what you just eloquently conveyed, Sayen. The RIGHTS Conversation Approach gives everyone a common way to engage in race dialogue. RIGHTS stands for *Respectful, Intentional, Genuine, Honest, Transparent,* and *Systemic.* Pamela will say more about this in her opening address, and you can also read about the approach and how it was developed in the digital summit program you all have access to via your phone. Speaking of Pamela, she's stepping up to the podium now." Stacey turned up the volume on the large monitor so everyone could hear what was happening in the main conference space.

A beautiful, slender, dark-complexioned Black woman with short hair and silver highlights stepped up to the podium. She looked around the room full of Black, Brown, and White faces. She had a warm but serious look on her face. She exuded power, dignity, confidence, and humility all at once. The audience sat in eager expectation of her words.

"Good morning everyone. Thank you for your presence at the third annual Having the Race Conversation Summit!" The audience rose from their seats with cheers and applause. After about twenty seconds, Pamela motioned the crowd to quiet down. "Thank you everyone. For those of you who have been with us since the beginning, you know the obstacles we faced to make this conference a reality and keep it going. In our first year, I lost my father to COVID-19. When we found out he was sick, I was going to cancel the summit. But he told me to keep going. Before he passed, he made me promise I would still carry out my work at the summit. He told me it was part of my purpose and that I would regret not following through on it when I got to be his age. By a show of hands, how many of you lost loved ones and people you know to COVID-19 over the last few years?"

Pamela paused and did a quick scan of the room. About ten percent of the audience raised their hands. Voices rose from the audience, saying "me," or "I did."

Many of the hands I see are disproportionately Black and Brown, which speaks directly to the inequities that still exist in our country. When my dad passed, I honored his wishes and pushed on with the summit, relying on the help of my family, friends, and team. When the media got wind of the summit, we got a lot of exposure, both good and bad. You may remember that in 2020, our former U.S. president banned diversity and inclusion training in federal government organizations. Many of you recall the heated exchanges he and I had over Twitter. While this was great publicity – that we couldn't have paid for, mind you – it led to death threats and a bombardment of hate messages against me. The threats and hate messages not only came from the usual suspects, White nationalists, but also from Black people who don't want us to succeed in our mission. This threw my team for a loop. But as I thought about our history as a nation, I realized this wasn't abnormal. Black people have often been used by White supremacy groups to subvert and dismantle Black led organizations that fight for the liberation of Black people. The FBI's COINTELPRO agenda, which was aimed against the Black Panther Party in the 1960s, is a clear example.

Still, we pressed on. I heard reports that the Brotherhood, one of many hate groups who stand against us, plans to hold a protest during the conference, outside the hotel. In response, we doubled our security and have local law enforcement on standby. You need not worry about your safety. It boggles my mind that people want to resist building stronger relationships across racial differences, but we will not let that stop us from accomplishing our mission," Pamela said.

At that, a man shouted from the back of the room. "We are with you Pamela!" The crowd erupted into more applause, shouts, and cheers. Pamela stood back from the podium for a moment with tears welling in her eyes. She was filled with emotion. After the crowd settled, Pamela continued. "Having the Race Conversation Summit has become more than an event. It is now a movement. Even though we are engaging in dialogue, we know this is only one part of dismantling systemic racism and oppression. The conversations we have here are a gateway to systemic change that is *sustainable*. This is why we added the S to our RIGHT approach, which I will now draw your attention to.

RIGHTS Approach
Respectful
Intentional
Genuine
Honest
Transparent
Systemic

We introduced this approach last year. Some of you are familiar with it. We wanted to field test it before we made it a central concept at this year's summit, so we commissioned a task force of over eighty professionals to try it out in their various fields of work, which span private and public sectors, academia, the justice system, and entertainment. These professionals were given the task of both practicing and inviting their organizations to try the RIGHTS Approach when discussing race.

First, they were to introduce this approach to their leadership teams. Then, they were asked to organize and lead a series of workshops around values corresponding to each letter in RIGHTS. This would give their organizations a solid foundation of knowledge surrounding the RIGHTS Approach, which would then help employees and leaders practice it in their day-to-day operations.

The results from participating organizations were significant enough for us to invest more, conduct further research, and devote more resources to partnering organizations. Some folks put their careers and reputations on the line to bring us valuable field data that validated the approach. We wanted you to know this is not some pie-in-the-sky theory. It has been proven, in the real world, to further the cause of Having the Race Conversation, which is ... say it with me y'all,"

Pamela paused as the crowd resounded in unison, "... to have effective conversations about race that lead to systemic change."

"That's right," Pamela continued, "now let's break this down so we can get a thorough understanding of how the RIGHTS Approach works. Let's start with the *R*, which stands for *respect*. Demonstrating respect is foundational to having effective conversations on race. Even if people disagree with one another, respect allows us to acknowledge each other as equals and the foundational commonality we all share, which is our humanity.

I stands for *intentional*. Having the race conversation takes intentionality. It is hard for many of us to face the ugly realities of what racism has produced, both within and outside of ourselves. The trauma some of us have been on the receiving end of because of race can make us want to tuck the pain deep into the recesses of our minds and hearts, never to see the light of day. Others may have intense feelings of guilt or shame because of the actions of their ancestors and the perpetual system of inequity they are privileged by. Therefore we all, no matter what perspective we hold, must force ourselves to engage in these difficult conversations. And after we hold these conversations, we must do our part to take action that dismantles systemic racism and establishes equity in its place.

G is for *genuine*. No one can afford to be phony in this work. While we want to be mindful of how we deliver our hard truths, we must be real and authentic in the ways we come to the table. If you don't agree with something someone says or an idea they have, be real about it. Don't fake the funk to get along. That will only cause more damage in the long term. But if we are genuine from the outset, we can get to the root of our issues quicker.

The next letter goes hand in hand with genuine. *H* is for *honest*. Being honest means being present in how we are feeling while we build bridges together. There will come a time in your racially inclusive journey when you get burnt out. Let me tell y'all, I quit every Tuesday," Pamela said with a light laugh. The audience laughed as well.

"In the spirit of honesty, diversity fatigue is real. And as much as I love people, working around different viewpoints and cultural backgrounds can make a sister tired," Pamela said as she rested against the podium.

"Preach, Pamela!" yelled another Black woman in the crowd.

"When discussing race, fatigue sets in because it takes an incredible amount of energy and effort to make what feels like only an inch of progress. The forcefield of White supremacy is so strong that it takes a massive amount of effort to penetrate it. I've spoken with countless White leaders of some of the nation's largest companies and institutions who, to the public, appear to understand racial disparities. But they haven't got a clue, nor the will, to disrupt the system.

On the other hand, you've got Black and Brown folks in high positions who benefit from this system and are afraid to change it from within. I was once one of those people. I spent decades climbing the corporate ladder, amassing wealth and notoriety for myself and stood quietly by while my brothers and sisters, not as fortunate as me, continued to be oppressed and left out of economic opportunity. I got to the point where I couldn't take it any longer. The spirits of my ancestors wouldn't let me sit idly by and do nothing.

So ya'll do me a favor right now, take off your diversity, equity, and inclusion superhero capes for a moment. We're gonna be respectful of each other while being honest about how we *really* feel. There's no way around this if we want to instigate systemic change. This is why we are handing out the Conversation Elephants this year. Everyone raise your elephants in the air. When you sense yourself tensing up because of a difficult conversation, breathe, and squeeze your elephant.

The next letter is the brother and cousin of the two letters before it. The *T* in the RIGHTS Approach stands for *transparent*. Racial conversations require us to be an open book about how the social construct of race impacts us and our worldview. This is a part of practicing being our authentic selves, which is why I had all of you take off your DEI capes.

Let me note that being genuine, honest, and transparent makes a bind of three chords that cannot be broken. By design, if you somehow manage to sneak past being genuine, honesty will catch you dead in your tracks. If you manage to slip out of honesty's grasp, transparency will tackle you down and force you to reevaluate yourself and others. Now, sometimes, we lie to ourselves and we get so good at it that we start to believe our lies. Transparency is meant to root that out so we can deal with the *real* us, which allows us to have truer dialogue across racial differences.

Finally, *S* stands for *systemic*. This value ties all the others together. If we don't get to the systemic nature of racism, then we are wasting our time. Those who have been oppressed because of the complexion of their skin are tired of talking. But they – we – keep coming back to the table in the hopes that doing so will move the needle of our society in the right direction. *Systemic.* The very nature of the word deals with systems. There are systems operating around us all the time. Systems are what keep families, communities, cities, and nations running so they can be healthy, happy and prosperous. The systems of race, however, were designed to advantage some and feed on others. Many believe we live in a broken system after seeing the latest headline about a Black person being killed by police and the White person who got away with it. I'd argue that in those cases, the system is operating exactly as it was designed to: those who have more pigmentation in their skin are not treated as human. Their lives are considered of little worth by racists who fight to keep the racial system, handed to them by their forefathers, in place.

Now, let's not get it twisted, the racial system is all about power and who controls resources. At a tribal level, we instinctively try to guarantee our chances of self-preservation. However, racism exacerbates this instinct through a doctrine of genetic superiority, seeking to subjugate all who don't share the same skin pigmentation. The concept of race as a genetic differentiator has been ripped to shreds and proven a fallacy by top scientists and academic minds, yet the concept of race as a social construct continues to run rampant and usually goes unchecked.

The tricky thing behind the systemic nature of racism is that it is a belief system, and many of us will die for a belief system if we think it is true. We can point to and change racist policy, but we can't necessarily change the minds of those who create those policies if they hold onto their racist beliefs. Racism persists because it has been deeply woven into our consciousness." Pamela paused to let the weight of her words sink in. "Because of this, we've got to be just as radical in our approach to unwinding the ancient chords of racist systems as those who continue to maintain them. This is why we place an emphasis on the *effectiveness* of the conversations we are having about race. We must weigh the conversations we are having against the intended result of systemic change. Systemic change occurs when the set of fundamental beliefs and protocols that govern racist systems get disrupted and a new, equitable pattern emerges.

The RIGHTS approach is not some cute little acronym, but a weapon of mass destruction aimed at racism. Every honest conversation you have today, all of which should be built on the foundation of respect and seeking to dismantle racial systems, is a potential bullet in our arsenal. Know that as you speak to one another today, your words have power and should be treated as such.

Now, let me say this: I understand there may be some who don't see what the big deal is about race. You may be thinking, 'we've made so much progress regarding race, especially with the election of the first Black president...' Side note: he is actually bi-racial, half White and half Black. 'And there are more Black people with higher-paying jobs and positions in public office than ever before.' So, we're past all of that racist stuff right? Wrong. Those who have been advantaged by racist systems often look at the progress that has been made, while those who find themselves marginalized by racist systems look at how far we still must go. Let's put it like this, if I stick a knife nine inches into your back, then pull it out six inches, is that considered progress? Absolutely not. In order to make progress, I need to pull the knife all the way out, drive you to the hospital, pay for your medical bills and any other work you may have missed due to the wound I caused you, apologize, and vow never to do you harm again. I'd argue that in the U.S., 'progress' looks like pulling the knife out two inches and putting rosy band aids around the wound and blade. We need to get the knife completely out so we can begin the long and arduous journey of healing.

In closing, I'd like to share my vision for living in a country where significant systemic change has occurred, pushing us toward sustainable racial equity. Because systemic racism is rooted in capitalism, it must also be addressed through capitalism. Capitalism is about ownership. Systemic change, from my perspective, involves a redistribution of wealth, power, and ownership to those who have been disenfranchised because of their skin color. This means that those who have been disenfranchised are provided with equitable opportunities for property ownership, business ownership, and financial ownership. We can accomplish this through a variety of elements: government programs, corporate wage programs, and banking programs. All three of these would be working both independently and in concert to ensure those who have been on the margins of U.S. prosperity are able to reap their fair share of the pie.

This could play out through significant numbers of people of color being able to purchase and maintain homes in predominantly White neighborhoods, providing proof that the racist practice of redlining is slowly being chipped away at.

Systemic change also looks like seeing more people of color in senior leadership roles at large companies. Often, the higher you go in an organization, the Whiter it is. We'll know we are making progress when we stop seeing the 'first Black person to sit on the board of company xyz,' or the 'first Latino to be CEO of an organization' in our LinkedIn feeds. While there is a first time for everything, we need to get to a place where we are seeing and experiencing the second, third, and forth instances of high-ranking executives being people of color. This will be part of the proof that we are dismantling racial bias within our companies.

Progress will be made when Black-owned businesses gain access to affordable loans and capital to help them grow in years of plenty, and sustain them in lean ones. Years down the road, these businesses will have the success necessary to be publicly listed on the Dow Jones, S&P 500, and the Nasdaq, should they choose to go that route.

When we begin to see wealth within Black households being handed down to the third and fourth generations, and we see this wealth increasing each year, we will know we are making progress."

Before Pamela could move on to her next point, a White man sitting on the far left of the room jumped out of his seat. "And what is the White man supposed to do? Sit idly by and watch his wealth and posterity dwindle away in his own country?" He howled like a dog, loud enough for the sound to fill the conference space, and ran out the doors before security could get to him. He had a Brotherhood logo emblazoned on the back of his black, faded jean jacket. The audience began to talk loudly amongst themselves. Somebody said above the din, "How did the Brotherhood get in here?"

Pamela motioned to the audience, asking them to quiet down after letting them talk amongst themselves for a few moments. "It's okay. We don't need to fear the Brotherhood. As a matter of fact, I welcome their raw point of view. You can't deal with what you refuse to talk about. This is precisely why we put a giant elephant in this room. We are not going to fall into the pattern of not dealing with racism. For those who may be on the fence about the necessity of having the race conversation, I hope that little outburst you just witnessed gave you a dose of reality. And you ain't seen nothing, yet."

Back in the green room, Derek felt his phone buzzing in his pocket. When he looked at it, he saw the CEO of Innovative Energy was calling him. He answered.

"Hey, this is Derek."

There was no response on the other end.

"Hello? Can you hear me?"

Again no response. He looked at his phone screen and saw he didn't have good cell reception. He got up to find better reception. Derek walked back and forth through the hallway, lobby, even the bathroom, but couldn't get a good signal to save his life. Looking at the clock, he knew breakout sessions were getting ready to start, but he couldn't wait any longer. He needed to hear from the CEO *now*. Desperate, he decided to go outside. He sped-walked through the long hallway, then started jogging when he got halfway to the entrance. He finally arrived at the front lobby and went outside. He covered his eyes as he stepped into the sun. When his vision returned, he saw that a large gathering of members of the Brotherhood had assembled just outside the hotel. Some of them had assault rifles and large American flags sticking out of their SUVs and trucks.

HTRC SUMMIT PASS

FOUR

OPEN CONFLICT

This is our country. It was built for us. If you don't like it, each and every one of you motherfuckers can go back to the shit holes you crept out of!" shouted a six-foot-three-inches tall, burly White man. The man had a red beard, dark sunglasses, and a red bandana tied around his bald head. He held a bull horn and appeared to be one of the chief agitators among the Brotherhood group gathered outside the hotel.

Derek stood still for a moment, about thirty feet from where the crowd was, calculating what his next move would be. He'd had skirmishes with other hate groups during his career, but this was more up close and personal, and guns were involved.

There were no police or security in sight. Although Derek was a polished professional, he normally carried a concealed firearm. But he hadn't thought about it today. He regretted that decision. As he stood just outside the hotel lobby doors, he felt the righteous indignation of four hundred years and counting of oppression his people suffered from the hands of racist White people. The Brotherhood was a reenactment of this history, only with new faces at the helm. A surge of anger overpowered Derek's temptation to tuck tail and run back into the hotel. Derek felt like this was a moment that would define him and he wanted to seize it. He knew his ancestors were watching. He knew standing his ground against these bigots could lead to one more notch on the belt of racial equity that his kids would carry when they became adults. He took a deep breath, removed his coat, and dropped it on a nearby car. He felt a thick bead of sweat run down his back. He was under no illusion of what was at stake: his life. Derek slowly walked in the direction of the leader of the Brotherhood.

The entire Brotherhood noticed him, appearing shocked by his audacity to approach them. The leader stopped mid-racist rant and revealed the large Glock 1911 pistol he had in the small of his back. Derek didn't break stride. He stopped fifteen feet shy of where they were. A deadly silence hung in the air.

After several seconds of this quiet standoff, the leader held up his bull horn. "What do you want, you Black bastard? Did yer little rainbow coalition convention run out of chicken?"

The Brotherhood erupted with laughter and hurled racial insults and slurs at Derek. Some even spat on the ground in his direction.

Derek said a silent prayer to himself that he had been using since his grandmother taught it to him when he was six years old. The Serenity Prayer. He said to himself, "Lord grant me the serenity to accept the things that I cannot change, the courage to change the things I can, and the wisdom to know the difference."

He squared his shoulders. "I respect your right to protest an event which you probably feel puts your future and the future of your kids at stake," he paused, looking as many of them in the eye as he could in that moment. "Hell, if the shoe was on the other foot, I might even find myself demonstrating with you. It's difficult to accept radical change, especially when that change doesn't seem to acknowledge you or your place in it. Racial equity, diversity, and inclusion all seem to be the latest craze. And even though well-founded data proves otherwise, it probably feels like White people in this country are getting the short end of the stick. It probably feels like there is a great deal of effort being put into amplifying the voices of people who look like me, while silencing yours. To some of you, it may even feel like a crime to be a White person who is proud of your heritage in this day and age. And perhaps you feel insulted that the status of Whiteness that your ancestors worked so hard to secure has become more and more tarnished."

The crowd of Brotherhood was still silent. Their eyes were locked onto Derek. He took this as a sign to continue. "We recently had a president in office who you might have felt voiced your concerns and moved with action on your behalf. And he was removed by the powers that be."

"Damn right!" yelled one of the Brotherhood members.

Derek searched for the man in the crowd. He was a skinny, middle aged man holding a rifle and leaning on a red pick-up truck. "So the question is, where do you go from here?" Derek continued. "The job market is more competitive than it's ever been, the demographics of this country are changing so rapidly that by the year 2050, you will no longer be the majority in this country. As intimidating as those firearms you all have are, they simply will not be enough to change the reality staring you right in the face."

"But it sure would feel good to shoot you and a bunch of others like you in the face!" said another of the Brotherhood members as he aimed his AR-15 at Derek.

"Lower your weapon, we can have civil discourse with his kind," said the leader to his trigger-happy comrade.

It took everything in Derek to not voice what was in his head. *I wish you would, you bitch-ass peckerwood!* Derek adjusted his disposition, knowing saying something like that would get him nowhere. "You could do that and it might make you feel good in this moment, but it isn't a great long-term strategy. More than likely, it will lead to your demise."

The man with the AR-15 scoffed, but lowered his weapon slowly.

"See, the thing is, the future isn't on the side of those who aren't willing to come to the table with people with racial backgrounds that they don't like," said Derek. "It just isn't how the world operates anymore. Even Grand Wizard Klansmen are having sit-downs with people they deem inferior to gain more perspective on the people they *have to* share the planet with. The days of purging the world of all non-White people are over. Globalization and social media have made sure of that.

"Since racism has become a global issue, those who entrench themselves in overt White supremacy will be left behind. Even White nationalists must evolve if they are to survive. That's probably a tough pill to swallow, but it's one to be gulped down nonetheless." Derek stopped talking and waited for a response.

The leader clapped, slow and deliberate. "Whooo, what a speech, you must be Obama's little brother. You really know how to captivate the crowd. I don't know whether to pump some hot lead into your Black ass or ask for an autograph."

"Now let me instruct you, since you've gone out of your way to inform us – uh, what do you people like to call us … ah, yes, rednecks – America was built on violence, necessary violence, that has produced many of the fruits we enjoy today. Not only physical violence, but psychological. Mental violence allowed our forefathers to carve out their own space and deem the White race superior to all. *All* dammit! It was *their* intestinal fortitude and know-how in the ways of war that put them in position to capitalize off America's greatest blessing to date. You know what that is, don't ya? Of course, you do. The *slave trade.*" The Brotherhood leader paused for a moment, rubbing his beard and adjusting his red suspenders. "Now, I know your kind feels like you have been treated unfairly, but I say you are looking at history with a glass-half-empty perspective. Had it not been for slavery, you wouldn't even be here, and you may not be having such a distinguished conversation with your *masters.*"

Derek could feel his blood boiling, like steam was rising off his head. But he refused to give-in to his urge to respond emotionally. He knew that was exactly what the Brotherhood wanted, and doing so would play right into their hands.

The Brotherhood continued their verbal assault and Derek began deep breathing exercises he'd learned about in a de-escalation training years ago from a former Navy Seal. He breathed in through his nose for four seconds and then exhaled for four seconds. He did this a few times until he was recentered and clear-headed.

"Hey, hey, you hear me boy?" yelled the Brotherhood leader.

Derek had tuned him out during his breathing exercises. "I'm sorry, can you repeat that?" Calm returned to him.

"Forget it! I think it's best you run along now before we go and fetch us a rope and string your ass up."

Derek, fully in-tune with himself and his surroundings, was not fazed. "You can try. But something you need to factor in before you act on your idle threats is that every time one of you kills one of us, our cause grows stronger while yours grows weaker. How else do you explain over sixty countries marching in protest in response to the death of George Floyd and others who have died unjustly at the hands of systemic White racism? Now, when I came out here, I tried to establish some common ground, but I see that is not possible based on your level of disrespect. So, let me drop some truth on you before I 'run along.'

The truth is, days are numbered for you and people who think like you. Many of you probably didn't make it through high school, so let me break this down into language you can understand: you and your kind won't be more than an afterthought in the future of this country. Will some form of your brand of racism still exist in the future? Sure. But it will not be tolerated. It will even be rejected by other White people who may secretly share some of the views you hold. How crazy is that? The people who resonate with you the most won't even claim you as their own. Here's why: smart White folks who are also racist have recognized that the social tide is shifting. Rather than try to fight it with rifles and good ol' fashioned lynchings, they are taking the smart route and choosing self-preservation. It will be political, professional, perhaps even physical suicide for them to associate with you. And because you will not be connected to their base of power, your influence will shrivel and die.

I live under no illusion that the U.S. is a racist country. I doubt that will ever change. But I am excited about seeing your branch of this racist oak tree become extinct, along with your grandiose visions of becoming a new Third Reich. As a matter of fact, your grandchildren have a high probability of entering romantic relationships with people outside of your race, making the ideologies you push look even more nonsensical. You don't even realize you are in a wave of change. You feel the disruption to your status quo, sure – otherwise you wouldn't be out here – but you don't understand its implications. I mean, you can't even publish your perspective on Facebook anymore! Now, let me leave you with this. Y'all finna get this work."

The Brotherhood members looked at one another, clearly puzzled about what he meant by 'work.' Derek heard one mutter, "Are we going to get our jobs back?" They didn't know "get this work" meant they were about to get a verbal smack upside the head.

Derek continued. "One *major* part of the equation I didn't mention about the unraveling of your ancient foothold is that Black people and other people of color have gotten wiser and stronger than you realize. We are more adept politically, financially, and socially than ever before and we have our own, formidable power bases now. So not only do you have to deal with people who look like you but are sick of your shit or pretending to be sick of your shit in public, but you also have to deal with *us*."

"You fucking nigger! Who do you think you are?" screamed an older White woman.

Derek was unphased by the racial slur. He thought for a moment, smiled, then replied. "I am my ancestors' wildest dream. I am a king. I am royalty. I am the offspring of the strongest people this world has ever known. I am the result of four hundred years of oppression and I still cannot be conquered. I am Black gold. I am the decider of what's cool in this country. I am Africa. I am America. I am a true patriot. I am the present form of the first humans to walk the earth. I am brilliant. I am the Africans who jumped off slave ships to take their chances with sharks rather than be subject to the chattel slavery system sanctioned by your dishonorable forefathers. I am the slave revolt of Haiti. I am a free man, a free Black man who speaks his mind. I am the soul of America. I am the culture that the world copies and tries to mimic. I am the Moors who taught your ancestors about medicine, math, science, and astronomy, helping them escape the dark ages. I am Mansa Musa, the richest man to ever walk the earth, a *Black* king, who made silver and gold as common as sand and rocks. I am the peaceful resistance of MLK. I am the armed resistance of Malcolm X. I am the unified strength of the Black Panthers. I am the embodiment of Maya Angelou's prophetic words, 'still I rise.' I am the entrepreneurial spirit of Black Wall Street and the captivating expression of the Harlem Renaissance. I am the patient warrior heart of Nelson Mandela who knew that justice would one day come for him and because of that, refused to bow to the Apartheid regime of South Africa. I am the melanin that is desired all around the world but despised by those who don't have it. I am the leader of humankind. I am the ancient people. I am the image of God."

Derek knew he needed to get back to the conference. He looked at his watch. "I'm also the keynote speaker for this conference and I need to get back. I'm sure they're wondering where I'm at."

"Not if I can help it" one of the Brotherhood members barked. He aimed his hunter rifle at Derek, the scope perfectly centered on Derek's head.

By this time a sizable crowd had formed around Derek and the Brotherhood.

A teenage activist, seeing the rifle pointed at Derek, yelled, "Bro! Look out!"

As soon as Derek heard the activist, he dropped to the ground, barely escaping the bullet that whizzed past his head and shattered a car window just behind him. People ran in all directions. Derek didn't move. He was in a state of shock and still face down on the ground. He had the sense to know there were more belligerent Brotherhood members nearby who still wanted to take a shot at him.

Just then, a police car pulled up. The voice of an officer, a White man, blared through the car's megaphone. "Is there a problem here?"

"No officer, just having a chat with our friend here," the Brotherhood leader responded.

Bystanders were recording the incident with their phones. Some yelled at the police officer, trying to get his attention. "The Brotherhood just tried to kill the Black guy over there! They need to be locked up."

Looking over at Derek, who was still lying on the ground, the police officer responded, "Hey let's try to keep the peace. I've been getting complaints about the noise." The officer drove past the crowd, giving a quick but noticeable salute to members of the Brotherhood.

"That's fucked up!" someone from the crowd yelled. "That cop clearly saw that brother get shot at!"

A young, freckled White woman ran to where Derek lay. "You need to hurry up and get back inside! It's not safe out here for you!"

Derek snapped back to reality. He pushed himself up off the concrete and ran inside. The remaining Brotherhood members left as well. Derek ran back into the hotel lobby and through the hallway, into an empty stall in the restroom. He was in a mental fog. The hotel staff looked oblivious to what just happened. They carried on with their work. *I almost got killed and no one in here has any idea what happened,* he thought. He thought about the countless Black bodies destroyed by racist violence and how they go unnoticed and uncared about. Derek was shaking from all of the adrenaline in his body. He felt so many different emotions that he wanted to yell at the top of his lungs. But somehow, he kept his composure. He went to the sink, washed his face, and took a few deep breaths before leaving the restroom.

As he approached the main summit conference room, he ran into a frantic Liz. "There you are! We've been looking everywhere for you! C'mon it's getting close to the keynote address. You can still sit in on a breakout session, for a few minutes, if you want, but we need to get moving."

Without glancing at Liz, Derek stared-off into the distance. "Sounds good."

BREAKOUT
SESSIONS

Breakout Session:
DO BLACK LIVES MATTER TO YA'LL YET?

"Which breakout session do you want to go to?" asked Liz as she sped-walked down the hallway. "There's about forty minutes left before we reconvene, so you may only be able to drop into one."

Still worn out from his experience outside, Derek did his best to not appear how he felt. It was a practice he learned to cultivate in his many years in corporate America.

"I'd be interested in *Do Black Lives Matter to Ya'll Yet*."

"Sounds good, I'll take you to the room it's being held in."

Derek could still tell she was upset with him from earlier in the day. When they got to the breakout room, with a tremendous amount of compassion that overcame his need to focus on himself, Derek extended an olive branch. "Hey Liz, I want you to know I realize I didn't handle the exchange between you and that racist hotel staffer correctly. I let you down in a moment when I could have been a true ally. I'm sorry."

Liz's demeanor remained professional, but Derek could see some of the tension she'd been holding melt away. "Thank you for acknowledging your mis-step. I know your heart was in the right place. We are all learning how to navigate these racial dynamics right?"

"Right," Derek said as he walked into the breakout room.

Inside, the air was tense. He grabbed a seat in the back to not draw attention to himself and his tardiness.

"All I'm saying is slavery happened before many of us were born. At some point, we have to get over it, right? Right? I mean what's done is done, we can only focus on *now*," said a short male attendee with glasses. The room went into an uproar as various hands shot up, requesting the mic to give their opinion. James motioned the crowd to lower the volume, but to no effect. People were talking amongst themselves. "Please everyone, I know we are all passionate about this, but let's be mindful of the noise level, and be respectful, so everyone who has something to say can be heard." James' tone was patient but firm. His voice commanded respect. The room quieted some.

Keisha, however, rolled her eyes and kept talking to the person she was sitting next to.

"The gentleman in the orange shirt, he was next," said James. The mic runner took the microphone to the man.

"I want to respond to the last guy's statement. I don't agree with, 'let's just get over slavery.' Slavery has impacted every facet of our existence in this country. You can't just get over something when it becomes a core part of who you are. Don't get me wrong, I am a free man. I am not a slave, but my ancestors were and the system we still live in here was very much built around the institution of slavery. I know many of us in this room, and at this summit, are trying to help rehabilitate America, but this is still the house that our enslaved ancestors built. We would be grossly negligent to forget that. I mean, do you see the Jewish community forgetting about and trying to get over the Holocaust? They say they remember the Holocaust so it will never happen again. And being that many of us still fall victim to the entrenched systems of racism that were birthed out of slavery, we would be wise to follow their example. And we don't even have to look that far to see that history has already been repeating itself right in front of us. Mass incarceration is hidden in plain sight. We represent thirteen percent of the U.S. population, but make up thirty-three percent of the sentenced prison population. White people make up sixty-four percent of the population but only thirty percent of those incarcerated. This is not an accident, people. Slavery was never abolished, it just moved locations. And the mainstream societal system is set up in a way to catch as many Black people, especially Black men, as they can to make us their slaves. I know some of us in here today echo Kanye's sentiment that slavery was a choice, but that statement was bullshit then and is bullshit now."

When the man finished his statement, the crowd erupted again. Some folks cheered and others raised their hands, eager to respond. James motioned to the crowd to lower the volume, but to no effect, again. A fire of passion had been lit and he realized he had to go in the flow of the momentum.

"Hey everyone, before we move to the next comment, I just want to re-center the group. What we are talking about is important and it needs space to continue. But for the sake of time, I want to make sure we address the original question, *do Black lives matter to folks outside of the Black race?* I want to make sure we are hearing viewpoints outside of our community. With that said, let's hear from the woman over there in the purple sweater."

The mic runner brought the microphone to a young Asian woman.

"Hi everyone," she said with her eyes toward the ground. "My name is Lindsey and my pronouns are she/her and I identify as Japanese American. I want to say I am grateful to be here today and hear all of your viewpoints around such an important topic, probably the most important topic our country is grappling with today. Not to put any feathers in my cap, but I've been to more Black Lives Matter protests than I can remember now. Me and some of my friends even started our own subset of BLM called Asians for Blacks. To be totally transparent with you all today and call me on my bullshit, if necessary, one thing I've come to realize is that the Black struggle in the U.S. is tied, almost foundationally, to the struggle of other racial minority groups here. Typically, when there are breakthroughs surrounding justice that happen for Black people in this country, other groups tend to benefit, as well. And when Black people are oppressed, it makes other groups more susceptible to similar oppression. Don't get me wrong, I'm not saying I've been protesting for Black lives for my own group to benefit. I've been doing so from a place of anger and frustration about the mistreatment you all have had to endure for so long. But I see the common thread and benefit of uniting together in your struggle, making it possible for the highway of justice to broaden for all marginalized communities. Thank you for hearing me out," she finished, taking her seat.

"Thank you for sharing that," said James. "Personally, your demonstrated commitment to our cause means a lot to me."

Derek could overhear quite a bit of lively discussion going on in room Clandestine, next door, where the breakout session about Reparations was happening. He decided to sneak out to better hear what was going on over there.

Breakout Session:
GETTING COMFORTABLE WITH THE R WORD, REPARATIONS

"All I'm trying to say is how can we prove who are the descendants of slaves and who aren't? It just seems like there's room for fraud and people abusing the system, getting benefits they don't deserve," said an older White man.

The racially-mixed crowd grumbled, some in agreement, others taking offense to the man's delivery. Derek stood at the edge of the room.

"Sir, I appreciate you sharing your point of view and your question. I'm sure there are many here who would like to address it. One thing I need to address, though, is your use of the word *slave*. It is preferable to use the words *enslaved people* instead. The Africans that were brought to this country through the Transatlantic Slave Trade were not slaves. Many were prestigious and noble people who fell prey to an inhumane, unjust, and cruel system," said Fatima. She was facilitating this breakout session. "With that said, does anyone care to respond before we move on?" She made eye contact with a woman at the back of the room with a raised hand. "Yes? Oh, please take the microphone to the young woman in the back, with the yellow sweater," Fatima said to the runner.

The mic runner brought the microphone to a young Black woman wearing her hair naturally with large gold bands on a braid. She wore large, white eyeglasses with gold accents.

"Thank you. When the global COVID-19 pandemic broke-out three years ago, the government quickly reached a deal to keep the American economy afloat. They dished-out money like it was going out of style to every man, woman, and child. There were hardly any hoops to jump through. Many of us received a stimulus check and other forms of government aid. The American government saw the plight of its citizens and responded in-time. During that time, I had a revelation. Whatever America decides to throw its weight behind, it will make happen. The reason we still don't see reparations for the descendants of enslaved African people, thank you for the language correction, Fatima," Fatima smiled at the front of the room. "is because America has decided it's not an issue worth caring about. If America truly cared about righting the wrong of chattel slavery and its generational effects, we would have seen the Fed and Congress break out their respective checkbooks and pay up. In the same way that you and I didn't have to jump through hoops to get our stimulus checks, the descendants of enslaved Africans brought to the Americas should not have to jump through hoops to receive our just due. Now let me say this, a check alone will not solve the generational mental, emotional, spiritual, and physical damage that has been done. But it would be a step in the right direction if it was connected to a comprehensive reparations program."

A number of people clapped and shouted in agreement while others shook their heads. Fatima, reading the room, said, "I see there is a mix of emotions and opinions as we discuss this topic. This is not something that's going to be solved in a ninety--minute session. But it is important that we are having this conversation. The young lady brings up a good point about the lack of hoop-jumping many people had to do during the COVID-19 Pandemic to receive aid. Yet many of the racially oppressed in this country have been seeking aid for centuries and it has not been honored. I know there are many of you here today who don't agree that reparations should be given to the descendants of enslaved people, but there are a number of you who do. Some of those who disagree feel this way because they don't see the benefit that distributed resources would provide. So, I'd like to shift the conversation to discussing what a successful reparations program could look like. Imagining this may give those of you who are resistant to the idea of reparations a vision that will make it more palpable. Let's see if we can do this exercise."

After Fatima said this, a handful of people got up and left the room. Fatima, ever the professional, was unphased by their actions, but she did squeeze her elephant behind her back.

"Great, those folks who left give us a round number of forty people. We can break up into five groups of eight. We are going to hand tablets to each group and when you write your ideas about what a successful reparations program could look like, they will show on the larger screen. We'll share out at the end. So, go ahead and self-select your groups. Please get up and move around the room and join a group of people you don't know."

As people stood up to form their groups, the room was silent. They were busy deciding which strangers they would sit with. People who vehemently opposed reparations were now grouping with people who were ardent supporters of it. Fatima watched with quiet glee as the process took place. She watched Derek join a group of mostly White women. He raised his hand to be handed a tablet.

People began to settle into their groups and make small talk. An interesting, collaborative energy took over the room. Instead of arguing for or against reparations, groups were putting their mental resources to work to come up with solutions. Fatima knew the power in the exercise was not convincing people whether or not they should support reparations. Rather, it was in getting people from different racial backgrounds to think about how to put a plan together as a diverse team. And maybe if people saw themselves as part of a team, despite their racial differences, they would also see themselves in the vision of a reparations program, instead of as outsiders.

Fatima knew that if given the chance, most people want to help others, even though fear creeps in when they don't know how to, or when they feel another group's gain is their loss. But being able to contribute in a meaningful way means just as much, if not more, as receiving the benefit of the contribution. Being able to contribute gives people buy-in. This is an aspect of human nature that often gets overlooked. Someone's need for significance, by way of giving, can outweigh their need to get something in return. She glanced at the ideas appearing on the screen.

🐘 *Don't require the descendants of the enslaved to pay taxes.*

🐘 *Create government sponsored programs that fund Black-owned businesses.*

🐘 *Launch a homeowner's program that provides Black people with a down payment they are not required to pay back.*

🐘 *Make it mandatory for Fortune 500 companies to hire a certain amount of Black people and stipulate that they hold a certain percentage of leadership roles.*

🐘 *Open up brokerage accounts for Black children and fund them until the recipients are 18 or 21.*

🐘 *Black people should get free healthcare, especially mental health care.*

Free college tuition for the descendants of enslaved people (and this should be funded by companies who profited from slavery).

Private K-12 education for the descendants of enslaved people.

A widely publicized apology from the Federal Government for the role it played in slavery, peonage, Jim Crow, Redlining, and police brutality, and an annual ceremony to commemorate these points in history, as a means to ensure we never repeat them.

Replacing confederate statues with statues of Black leaders and influencers who fought against and resisted slavery, and who made significant contributions to society.

Change school curriculum to reflect an accurate depiction of slavery, and to show who Black people were prior to slavery. Emphasize the contributions they've made to America since then.

Create federally sponsored technical training programs specifically for Black people who want to work in the tech field.

Mandate that publicly traded companies publish yearly salary reports by racial demographic.

The screen filled up as ideas flooded in. The creative energy in the room was mesmerizing, although there were still some who demonstrated their disapproval with folded arms, indifference, or clear displays of being disinterested. But the momentum was on the side of those from various racial backgrounds who were working together to come up with ideas for how reparations could be implemented in the twenty-first century.

Breakout Session:
WHITE PEOPLE ARE DIVERSE, TOO

Kevin hit his stride. He continued his discourse to the sea of mostly White faces staring back at him. "Often, we White people don't consider our ethnicity of origin. But many of our ancestors were immigrants who came to the U.S. to find opportunity. In some of the older cities in the nation, such as New York and Boston, you can still find European Ethnic enclaves that highlight the differences in 'Whiteness.' Some of these enclaves include dense pockets of those who identify as Albanian, Croatian, German, Hungarian, Greek, Irish, Italian, Jewish, Polish, Russian, Serbian and Ukrainian.

Many of us have been in the U.S. for generations, or long enough that our country of origin does not make much of a difference in how we experience life here in the U.S. anymore. That puts us at a disadvantage in the race conversation because if we don't understand our differences, we cannot appreciate the uniqueness of others who differ from us, especially racially. Even if we don't have a full understanding of our ancestry, we still need to do our work to understand how the learning and actions of our ancestors has shaped the way we view the world today. Knowing more about our origins will help us move a little further outside of the comfort zone of Whiteness, and may allow us to build more impactful bridges with people from different racial backgrounds and ethnicities. It's time we go a little deeper into our own narratives and see beyond the thick veil of Whiteness. Whiteness has a horrible brand right now, but I believe we can reshape it into something good as we explore our stories, do the work necessary to challenge and overcome our biases, and use the influence we have to dismantle oppressive systems.

I think one of the first steps is to realize that White people are diverse, too. Away with this notion that Whiteness is a monolith. Outside of our various ethnic origins, we are diverse in opinion, social-economic status, political beliefs, faith traditions, and life experiences, among so many other things. As we explore our differences, we develop important muscles that cultivate curiosity. This curiosity can lend itself to helping us appreciate and celebrate the differences of those of other racial backgrounds.

For some of us, exploring aspects of our Whiteness can be daunting. Some of us have family histories we may not be proud of, histories that induce shame and guilt. When I first found out that my great grandparents owned enslaved people and the plantations they worked on, I had a hard time accepting it. I was depressed for weeks. It's sometimes easy to forget that slavery in the U.S. was declared unlawful only one hundred and fifty years ago. This reality has made me confront the truth about the foundations on which my "good life" has been built.

On the other side of this, my family-origin story has not been only dark. My ancestors were brave settlers who came to the U.S. and were hardworking planters who secured a legacy that my family and I enjoy to this day. What I am getting at here is that our stories are complex, wide ranging, and meaningful. In them, we find our cultural similarities as well our most fundamental differences.

"Enough of me talking, though. Let's jump into some Q&A," Kevin finished. "First question from the gentleman with the white hair and black shirt."

"Hi. Uh, yes. I appreciate what you shared with us today. I guess my question is, shouldn't we be more focused on minorities and their stories? It seems to me like much of the narrative in the U.S. has been about us White people. Wouldn't focusing on our in-group diversity preclude us from exploring other groups' diversity on a deeper level? Thanks."

"That's a great question. In this case, it's a *both-and*. We have to do our in-group work while we also work at deepening relationships across groups. One of the chief ways we can dismantle the myth of White superiority is by seeing how different we all are within the umbrella of Whiteness. The term White tends to perpetuate this notion of rightness, but we've got some pretty messed up shit to get straight amongst ourselves. I believe that facing sobering facts will help us get down from our White horses, pun intended, and get to work. Also, as we do our work, we position ourselves to use some of those same skills toward leaning into the stories of people of color. Does that answer your question?" asked Kevin.

"Yes it does, thank you."

An older Black woman in the middle row raised her hand to speak. The mic runner brought the mic to her face but she waved them away. "Can everyone hear me?"

Almost everyone nodded their heads yes.

"I don't think I need the mic, honey," she said to the mic runner. She paused as she looked around the room, making eye contact with some of the people there. She was one of the few Black people in the room. "I was debating on whether or not I should share my thoughts, given this particular breakout session is about *your* work that *you* must do as White people. But listening to some of the conversations that have gone on, I decided I'd be remiss if I didn't share my perspective, as a Black woman, on what you all are discussing. Now, I'll be seventy-two next month and I've gotten to the age where I call it like it is. I don't have the length of years left to beat around the bush.

That said, my polite side would say I commend you all for being here to engage in conversations about race. However, my real side, my soul, the side of me who lived through the Jim Crow Era, the side that saw my daddy get treated like he was a little boy when he was a full-grown man with a family, the side that had to bury my twenty-four-year-old grandson because a police officer shot him to death because he thought my grandson was reaching for a gun when he was reaching for his ID, the side of me who has seen the trees where they lynched thousands of Black bodies for sport and entertainment, the side of me that both witnessed and felt the impact of home ownership inequality and gentrification, the side of me who knows how much progress thas been made in this country regarding race relations but is all too aware of how far we still have to go before we are all treated as equals ... this is the side I will speak to you from today.

As you all explore the diversity amongst yourselves, which is important, I hope you don't linger on that for too long. I feel that if you prolong your stay on this subject, it will become yet another tree to hide behind in the forest of racism. Don't get me wrong, demystifying Whiteness is important because racism was of your creation, therefore you should play the largest role in dismantling it."

When she said this, she saw a few people looking down and others folding their arms. Reading the room, she responded, "If what I'm saying hurts, say ouch, but I'm going to keep going. The innocent blood of my grandson demands me to. The humiliation and emasculation of my father demands me to. And the fact that they still have not received justice, demands me to! Remember, it was not that long ago, only a couple years, when White terrorists stormed the nation's capitol to block the peaceful transfer of power between presidents. Armed and violent, they waltzed through congressional halls virtually unchecked. Had that been Black militants, there would've been a massacre. The message that was sent to all Black people has not been lost on me. Even the most brutal forms of Whiteness will be treated better than the most peaceful forms of Blackness. As you all discuss the diversity amongst yourselves, I hope it will be with this in mind." The woman then took her seat.

After a long and awkward silence, Kevin responded. "Thank you for your candid feedback and for sharing those very personal experiences. My heart hurts hearing what you lost due to systemic racism. It is also painful to know there are so many more stories like yours, which I've heard from several other Black Americans. These stories should not be the norm, but shamefully, they are. I fully agree that we, as White people, need to get better at and welcome the process of decentering ourselves without abdicating the work we need to do within our group. Your perspective and that of the gentleman who spoke before you helped me frame the questions I want us to consider in our small groups."

In what ways can those of us who identify as White, identify, understand, and celebrate our unique ethnic and cultural diversity?

"I'd like to add to that question, how can we do this in a way that lends itself to better understanding and celebrating individuals of other racial backgrounds?"

How can we use the diversity within Whiteness to deconstruct and dismantle the negative aspects of Whiteness?

"I'd like to replace the word *negative* with *racist*. Let's call a spade a spade here."

Some people's faces turned red, others stared at Kevin like deer in highlights. Kevin knew this was a good sign that growth could occur here.

"I want to share something before I have you all get into your breakout groups again. I've often said that pain is a necessary component of transformation. It's human nature to fall into complacency when we become too comfortable. I've seen the discomfort on many of your faces today as we have talked about owning our own diversity, as well as addressing the racism that's all around us. I want you to use this discomfort to lean into the unknown, now more than ever. On the other side of that discomfort, you will find a powerful transformation awaiting you. Some of you may be asking why this transformation is even important. For me, it comes down to being able to look at myself in the mirror. I want to see and understand the full picture of who I am, and part of that means becoming more than what my ancestors were, especially as it pertains to being racially inclusive."

Kevin paused as he tried to hold back tears welling in his eyes. After he gathered himself, he said, "Really, this is about the human soul. How much of a soul can you have when you become aware of the oppression of others due to their skin color and then not do something about it though it is in your power to act. It baffles my mind how we, as White people, can continue to live in and tolerate such a destructive system, one which is robbing people of opportunity, their mental and physical health, and their very lives and the lives of their loved ones. I know I'm preaching to the choir but..."

"You ain't preaching to no goddamn choir. What you are is a fucking traitor!" interrupted a White man who stood up abruptly before storming out of the room.

"Apparently, there are more Brotherhood members here who have infiltrated the conference. Nevertheless, we push forward. I hope this was confirmation for those of you who are still on the fence about dealing with your own racism and those of our own kind. This will be a great point of further discussion during lunch."

LUNCHTIME

Groups of people began to pour into the large banquet room. The tables inside were set with shimmering, gold-colored eating utensils laid on cloth napkins and table coverings. The floral center-pieces were bursting with color inside crystal vases.

Facilitators and speakers had their own table near the stage. Before most of them could take their seat, they were stopped by summit participants to further elaborate on their respective breakout sessions. Derek, who was normally very social, arrived at the table first. He was hungry and still shaken from his encounter outside, with the Brotherhood, though most of the participants seemed oblivious to the entire episode. Derek was still concerned about his career with Innovative Energy, too. It weighed heavily on his mind.

He pulled out his phone and scrolled through his LinkedIn feed as a distraction from the noise around him.

Before he went too deeply into thought, Liz tapped him on the shoulder.

"Hey Derek, are you alright? You seem like you've been a little unplugged from the summit since the breakout sessions…"

Instantly, Derek came to himself. "You know Liz, I almost lost my life an hour ago and no one seems to have noticed. Even at a summit like this, which should be a safe space for people to explore racial differences, my life and well-being are still threatened. It's just a trip, you know?"

"Wait a minute, did you just say you almost lost your life?! As in, you were almost killed? How…Who?"

"Yep, just outside, I got into a confrontation with the Brotherhood. They pointed their guns at me, then shot at me … the whole nine. A police officer came to the scene and didn't even bat an eye at them. He let them all go. It just happened, during the breakouts."

"Oh my God, Derek! Did you report this to anyone?"

"I didn't get a chance to. I think you're the first person at the summit who knows about it. Which is crazy because there was a big crowd outside watching the whole altercation. You would think by now it would be on social media … It almost feels like the whole thing was planned. I'm not trying to go too deep down a conspiracy theory-hole, but I don't think it's too far-fetched to believe it was planned, considering the Brotherhood has infiltrated the summit."

"You're right. Piecing it all together makes me realize there were several incidents involving the Brotherhood today. At first, I just ignored them and thought it was part of the price of doing this work. But there may be something much deeper at play here. We need to let Pamela and her team know so they can be prepared, just in case there's another attack."

"Let's do it," Derek said. They both stood up and headed to where Pamela was seated.

About twenty feet away, Sayen was engaged in a deep conversation about her breakout room session, *Exploring Today's Indigenous Narrative,* with a White summit attendee.

"Thank you for being so transparent and open about your story, Sayen. So much of my perspective about Native people was formed through movies like Pocahontas and Dances with Wolves and I ignorantly made many assumptions about indigenous people as a result. You blew my mind when you shared that the U.S. Constitution was largely inspired by the Haudenosaunee Confederacy. That reminded me how much I don't know in the world and makes me want to learn more about Native people," said the summit attendee.

Sayen couldn't help but smile from ear to ear. "I'm glad you got something out of today's session. Pop culture has really had a negative impact on Native people, even internally. It has caused a loss of tradition that many young Native people are working hard to regain. A lot of young people don't know their tribal languages because of the lure of video games, tv, and trying to be cool in mainstream society. But as they get older, we do see youth realize the power of knowing who they are through connecting to their people."

"It seems like that's something most cultures and racial groups have in common: trying to reinforce the importance of tradition and cultural values for the next generation while competing against modern distractions. I have a ten-year-old son who is Velcroed to his iPhone. I do my best to make him put it away when we have family time, but it's a struggle. Although you and I come from different racial backgrounds, I can relate to the importance of trying to maintain traditions that might help my son find his way when he's older."

"Yeah, the struggle is very real. We all feel it, regardless of our racial and ethnic background. I became passionate about the traditions of my ancestors when I realized many of the symptoms I saw in young Native people, such as alcohol and drug abuse, were directly linked to intergenerational trauma and genocide. Early European settlers tried to strip us of our culture and identity by beating, raping, and killing our bodies and spirits. I feel like reconnecting to our traditions and ceremonies is a strong way to help us heal." Sayen said with tears welling in her eyes.

"I can tell you are helping a lot of people, Sayen. I admire you."

"I appreciate the kind words. I'VE resolved to do my part. One of the most important decisions I ever made was to heal myself and break the cycle of destruction for generations of Natives coming after me. I want them to know that after all we've been through, we are still full of energy, life, and creativity. We are still here!"

After that, the two embraced and went to find their tables. Across the way, Alex and another White woman were engaged in what appeared to be open debate.

"Oftentimes, we White women don't recognize our power. In many instances, we are given the benefit of the doubt even if we're clearly in the wrong. Black women and Latina women are not afforded the same luxury," Alex said as the other White woman nodded in agreement. Alex continued. "I remember, there was a time – not long ago – when I was afraid to talk about race and Whiteness. I was scared I might say the wrong thing, cause hurt, and offend people."

"That's where I'm at right now," replied the other White woman. "It's a big reason I'm at this conference. I need to conquer my fear of discussing race. How did you get so comfortable talking about it? You seem so confident."

"To be honest, even to this day, I still get a little fearful," said Alex. "But I've had so much practice that I'm able to rely on the muscles I've built around having awkward conversations about race.

I had an epiphany when Breonna Taylor was murdered. I realized I couldn't let awkwardness stop me from playing my part and speaking up about racial injustice. I didn't necessarily know what to say, but I knew I had to say something. That's really how it starts. You gain an awareness that something is wrong, and then just say something about it. To this day, I still get it wrong sometimes, but everybody does. That's part of being human and learning from your mistakes so you can keep improving."

"I never thought about it like that. I always feel that if I say the wrong thing, that would be the end for me. I'd be labeled a racist and no one would want to associate with me."

"That's a very common fear that many of us have. We don't want our misspeaking to be seen as perpetuating the system of White privilege. But this does more harm than good. We have to be honest with others about where we are at in our journey and keep practicing, just like anything else we want to become good at," said Alex.

"Can you tell me more about your views on White privilege? It's a concept I sort of struggle with. I feel like I've worked hard to get everything I have. I didn't come from a rich family and I've earned every achievement I made the hard way," said the other White woman.

"White privilege is a concept I used to struggle with, too. I didn't come from a wealthy family, either, and I have busted my ass to get where I'm at. But as my eyes began to open more and more to the reality of our society, I saw that White privilege is real. It's a system geared toward White people succeeding at the expense of others. It's not that White people don't have to struggle to succeed, it's that our Whiteness isn't an impediment to our success while the skin color of others can be. People of color often succeed *despite* their skin color, whereas with White people, our Whiteness is usually an *asset* because of how our society is set up."

"That makes a lot of sense. You're right, I've never really had to think about my Whiteness as a factor in everyday life. Nor have I thought about how it may have made things easier for me. I really pride myself on being color-blind when it comes to race. I just see people as people, regardless of their skin color. I mean, why can't we just focus on what we have in common instead of our differences, right?"

Alex waited a moment before responding, not wanting her tone to come off judgmental. She knew that was one of the quickest ways to lose a person when there is aa difference of opinion. "You know, color blindness can be a bit of a slippery slope, especially when we apply it to people of color. I can share more if you'd like to hear it," said Alex, knowing that gaining permission to share a contrary belief was an effective strategy for that belief to be heard instead of resisted.

"Please do, I'm intrigued."

"Okay, well when someone practices color blindness, what they will probably miss is the suffering that a person's skin color might cause them. In effect, it invalidates that suffering. Not intentionally of course, but the impact of that invalidation greatly outweighs the intent of viewing everyone the same. Color blindness, in theory, is a good idea. But in practice, it doesn't work because of the reality of racism that people of color face everyday. The term I've adopted, which came from Mellody Hobson, is "Color Brave." Color Brave is when we see the color of everyone we engage with and celebrate the difference between us. Instead of pretending I don't see it in an effort to treat everyone equally, I fully embrace that aspect of their identity, account for the challenges others may face as a result of that identity point – as much as I'm able to – and do my part to treat people with the same amount of dignity and respect that I expect in return.

And in all honesty, it just makes my relationships across races easier. Black women can smell our bullshit a mile away, so we might as well be upfront about our hang-ups when it comes to race," Alex said.

The other White woman let out an uneasy laugh as she processed the information Alex just shared with her. She believed so deeply in the philosophy of colorblindness that it was hard to accept Color Braveness as the correct philosophy. She had been taught as a young girl to treat everyone the same. Growing up, and throughout most of her adult life, she had little interaction with Black people and other groups outside her race.

"I don't know. I thought the whole racial equality thing was about everyone getting the same treatment. I mean, isn't that what Dr. Martin Luther King's dream was all about? I strive to be inclusive of everyone and focus on our similarities. We can find similarities if we look hard enough," the other White woman said.

Alex paused again, then said something she knew could help her win the argument but potentially lose the person. "The main issue with treating everyone equally is that it assumes everyone has an equal playing field in life. Can someone hope to win the game when the part of the field they are in is filled with quicksand? That person would need a different kind of support, or treatment, to succeed. That person is just as capable as other people on the field, but the conditions they find themselves in require that they be treated differently in order to play at their full potential. Does that make sense?" Alex asked this with as much empathy and care as she could muster.

"I guess I see where you're coming from. I just think that if I was a Black person, I wouldn't want to be treated differently because of my skin color."

"But that's part of the issue we White women have. We can't ever know what it's like to be a Black person, so we can't assume we know what they want or how they want to be treated." Alex was a little annoyed now, but she tried to remain engaged in the conversation.

"I get that, but I think everyone has a basic need to be treated with respect and kindness. And that is universal. I feel like as long as I do that, people of all racial backgrounds will feel included around me," the other White woman said. Her tone matched Alex's level of annoyance.

Alex, tapping into her high level of emotional intelligence, understood that the conversation had the potential to go off the rails at that moment. Although she knew racial inclusion was a lot more involved than the other White woman made it out to be, she realized she didn't need to convert her to her own way of thinking. She remembered that inclusion is a journey, not a destination, and everyone needed to find their own path.

Alex took a deep breath and responded. "I think you are on the right track. There's so much to learn about racial inclusion, I'm sure we could stand here for a lifetime discussing it. But I think the food is getting ready to come out. You hungry?" Alex asked in a lighthearted tone.

The White woman, looking somewhat confused, said, "yes, I most certainly am. But I have one more thing to ask you about, if you don't mind."

"Of course, lay it on me," Alex said.

"The other day, when I was at the grocery store, I was in the middle of a disagreement with one of the cashiers, and the person behind me in line called me 'Karen.' My name is Sally. Why did they call me Karen?"

Alex smiled, "It's a long story..." and proceeded to tell the woman the history behind the label "Karen."

Not too far from them, Zhang was in a deep conversation with a Vietnamese American man about his breakout session, *The DEI Revolution, or the Status Quo in Disguise.*

"It's my opinion that a lot of this DEI stuff is the status quo in disguise. I'm all for diversity and inclusion, heck my parents came here as refugees after the Vietnam War. They were able to assimilate into society and create opportunities for my brothers,sisters and me, but we had to work our butts off to get where we are today. Although we were welcomed here in the U.S., nothing was handed to us. Now, all of the sudden, DEI is the hot topic and everyone wants to run around talking about how inclusive they are. To me, it's horseshit. We were treated badly before the Coronavirus. Now, we are treated worse. Even some of the people at this conference, which is supposed to be focused on racial inclusion, look at me funny. A lot of these people know the jargon of DEI work, but it isn't real to them in their heart and mind. I feel like a lot of them are profiting off teaching DEI related topics but are not truly 'walking the walk' behind closed doors," said the Vietnamese man.

A skilled listener, Zhang listened to what the man was saying without forming a response. He was listening to understand before he sought to be understood.

"At the end of the day, what matters most in this country is money," continued the man. "And I feel that behind all of this DEI stuff, there's a bunch of rich White people profiting just like in every other industry. Sure, I want to be treated more fairly and not be discriminated against because I'm Vietnamese, but I know how this country works. The more money you have, the more options you have. It's that simple. And I'm not mad about it. My parents told me how hard life was in Vietnam. They swear that this government is the best in the world. That's why they voted for Donald Trump in the last election. To them, he represents freedom and democracy.

Many older people in my community feel the same way, too. But I don't. Personally, I think the guy is a sleazeball. I tried to convince them that he wouldn't be a good president. But their minds were made up."

"Yes, I heard something about that," Zhang said. "The Vietnamese were the only Asian American group to support Trump more than Joe Biden. Why do you think that was?"

"It's pretty simple. The older generation, who came here after the Vietnam war, were convinced that Donald Trump was pro-democracy. They never want to experience communism again, and they felt like Trump was a president who could guarantee that. There's a big divide on this issue between older and younger generations. I spent a lot of time trying to convince my parents to vote for Biden, but their minds were made up. In some ways, I can understand their position. When you go through a substantial amount of trauma, you will latch onto anything that seems like the opposite of what you've experienced."

Zhang chimed in. "I definitely agree. I think that's why so many Chinese Americans work hard to blend in here in the U.S. They feel like blending in might mitigate some of the discrimination we face, giving us a chance to be seen as equals. But COVID-19 revealed that no matter how hard we work to assimilate, we are still seen as different, as *other*."

"Especially when you had the most powerful man in the country, if not the world, calling COVID-19 'the Chinese Virus.' That just emboldened closet racists to act more boldly on their beliefs. I remember when we only got made fun of by comedians because of our dominance in the nail care industry. But ever since the pandemic started, it's been open season for violence against the Asian American community," said the Vietnamese man.

At that, both men just stood in the solemness of that reality. After the silence became unbearable to him, Zhang, in his extroverted style, broke the spell. "Can I ask you something I've always wondered about Vietnamese Americans? It's something you just touched on?"

"Yeah, sure," the Vietnamese man shot back.

"How *did* the Vietnamese become so dominant in the nail care industry? Oftentimes, people who are not Asian think all or most Asians have a stranglehold in that industry, but it's you all." Zhang hoped he had built-up enough trust with this person to ask such a direct question related to ethnicity.

The Vietnamese man let out a soft laugh. "It's actually kind of random. Have you heard of the Hollywood actress Tippi Hedren?"

"She was a little before my time, but the name rings a bell," replied Zhang.

"Well, after the Vietnam War, Tippi was a strong supporter of Vietnamese refugees to the U.S., especially women. She had about twenty women who she would hang out with who she also hired to help manage her estate. They were enthralled by her fancy nails, so she had her manicurist teach them how to do their nails the same way. That's where it all started. Those twenty women took that knowledge and ran with it. Also, because you don't have to speak good English to do nails, many Vietnamese women and men were able to get into the business fairly easily. Forty years after the fall of Saigon, the stats are that fifty-one percent of all nail techs here in the U.S., and eighty percent in California, are of Vietnamese descent."

"Wow, you learn something new every day. That is a powerful story. That sounds like an origin story everyone should know about. Knowing the history behind things like this greatly humanizes people," Zhang said.

"I think so, too. When I tell people about this, they always say the same thing. I also get a lot of people who apologize for the stereotypical jokes they've said about Vietnamese nail techs in the past. Sharing history and stories, I feel, are the gateway to building connections across differences. We can identify with many aspects of another person's story and history if we are willing to slow down, be curious, and absorb a new experience," said the Vietnamese man.

Almost cutting him off, Zhang jumped in. "Exactly! The vulnerability and authenticity we exhibit when we share our history and stories create a magnetic connection. From there, I think we can lead people to make investments into systemic change. They just have to be exposed to the experiences of others."

"Can I chime in for a second?" asked an unfamiliar voice. "I'm sorry, I'm really not trying to hijack your conversation, but I haven't been able to stop ear hustling," said an multiracial woman who appeared to be in her mid-fifties but could easily pass for someone younger.

"Absolutely, please," said Zhang and the Vietnamese man.

"After doing this work, the work of DEI, for almost four decades, I'm convinced that sharing our stories and backgrounds is not sufficient for radical change within oppressive power structures. I may be a little jaded, but I'm not even sure if it's a good starting point," the woman said. Her presence felt warm and kick-ass at the same time.

Zhang, who was at first mesmerized by her beauty, was now in a state of shock from her comment. Her ideas were in direct conflict with his last statement and his overarching paradigm. He came to himself. "Please, say more."

The woman continued, "What I've found is that as you mentioned, all the magnetic sparks fly when people of different races connect through their stories, struggles, identities, and all the et ceteras. At the end of it all, people give each other fist bumps, hugs, high fives, and post a picture on social media, looking like a miniature version of the United Nations with a caption about what a great time they had... They learned so much... They found their long-lost brothers and sisters... yada yada yada on their Instagram and LinkedIn profiles. But after that, most of the DEI committees and councils they formed, if they even get off of the ground at all, start languishing from discontinued interest, commitment, funding, or organizational support. Then, many of the people who are in those committees and councils become frustrated because they had high expectations of what they would accomplish, only to have those expectations dissolve before any impactful work can take place.

I've seen this cycle over and over again. There are elements that have to be put into place to ensure the heartfelt stories shared and connections made turn into sustainable action over the long term. DEI is a long term investment that may not yield returns for several months, maybe even years. And when I speak of returns, I'm not talking about good feelings after a workshop, I mean tangible evidence of shifts in workplace culture in terms of how people are treated, especially people of color.

Among people of color, Black people are the litmus test for how inclusive a workplace culture is. Cultures don't change from a single workshop or training. Those are just tools to help cultures along. Lasting organizational change comes from leadership making a decision to get behind, inspire, and enforce change."

Zhang and the Vietnamese man took mental notes. They both knew she was telling the truth. Out of curiosity, and a bit of ego, Zhang asked, "Okay, but in your experience, how do you go about bridging racial divides in corporate spaces?"

"Whether it is in a private or public space, leadership has to be willing to commit their budgets and influence to building those bridges. They must regard racial inclusion as just as important as sales, technology, finance, research and development, and so forth. If they don't, even the best designed program and initiatives will die before they have a chance to produce fruit. The pay off comes when all or most employees are developed to reach their potential. A company where this is the case is unstoppable. They will have a deeply dedicated and skilled workforce who provides top-of-the-line service for their customer bases.

A big question many executive leadership teams need to answer is why they don't have more people of color, specifically Black people, at the top of the house. The lower you go in an organization, the more melanin you will find. The higher you go, the less you find. Once leadership teams answer this question and face the messy truth, they can get to work. When people of color, especially Black people, are in seats of power, well resourced, and supported by the organization, that will begin to shift dynamics and bridge the racial divide in the private and public sectors. Get the right people on the bus, then you can begin to drive toward the destination.

Many organizations put the cart before the horse, though. They try to begin DEI work without understanding why the racial demographic of their leadership looks the way it does. From my experience, many organizations are not ready or willing to change the racial make-up of their executive teams. I work with a lot of Fortune 500 companies, and something I proposed to my clients, who say they are ready to start changing their culture to be more racially inclusive, is that they must develop a strategic plan that will lead to at least fifty percent of people on their leadership teams bepeople of color, specifically Black people, within eighteen to thirty-six months. I've worked with over fifty different, large scale companies, and only one took me up on that suggestion. But the company who did saw an almost immediate improvement in workplace morale, retention, and productivity.

That's not to say that they didn't have their struggles along the way. Even to this day, they still face pushback. But they chose to struggle in a direction toward progress instead of complacency. Their leadership made the decision to truly live out the values they wrote about in their press releases and on their website after George Floyd's murder.

A lot of companies get stuck in their racial inclusion initiatives because they don't make a real decision about how to carry them out. They mistake making a decision about them with addressing something that is currently happening. Once you make a decision, you are committing to a course or courses of action over an indefinite period of time, not just committing to showing solidarity when the latest headline or hashtag is trending. Addressing something, while sometimes noble, is fleeting because it focuses on a single event that will soon fade into the background.

This is where ninety percent of the companies I work with fall. Their commitment to racial equity is *reactionary* when it should be *proactive*. My field of specialty is helping some of these same companies move from reaction to response and from procrastination to provocation."

"Interesting word choice, why provocation?" asked Zhang.

"Because in order to see movement, a lot of these companies – who have gotten good at practicing racial bias over decades – need a swift kick in the ass to get going. But there's an art to it. If you push people too hard, they'll resist; but if you go too easy on them, they won't take things seriously. So, my job is to provoke them into action. I carry this out in a variety of ways, but my main tactic is to be honest with them about how they've screwed up and how they can course-correct. Clients who are ready to make a change often welcome this approach."

"I'd love to chat more with you about this," said Zhang. "You have a well of knowledge about it, and your no-nonsense approach is refreshing. That's something I want to adopt. It looks like they're bringing out the food … can I grab your card before we get to our seats?"

"Please give me one, too. I want to keep in touch," said the Vietnamese man.

"Most certainly." The woman reached into the large bag she carried on her shoulder. She pulled out two business cards and handed them to the men. She smiled at them, "Great talking to you both. I hope I didn't take over your conversation too much. That really wasn't my intent."

Zhang, not wanting to reveal his blossoming crush on her, said, "No, we enjoyed the conversation! I got a lot out of it. Here's my card as well, I'd love to stay in touch."

"I don't have a card to give you, but I just followed you on LinkedIn, I'll reach out to find time when we can talk again." The Vietnamese man finished.

"Sounds like a plan, you both enjoy the rest of the summit and your day," the woman said with a glimmer in her eye.

At the front of the banquet hall, Pamela was finishing up her conversation with Liz and Derek. "We are going to settle this right now," she said as her nostrils flared. Still, she remained poised. She stepped up to the podium, which was just a few feet away from them.

"Testing, testing. Can you all hear me?" Several people from the audience gave her a thumbs up.

"It has just come to my attention that the Brotherhood has set up a significant presence here at this year's summit. And you know I wouldn't discourage that if they truly wanted to understand what it is we do and talk about here. I believe this provides an opportunity for bridge building. But what will not be tolerated here are threats and violence. One of our key people in this year's summit just told me they were shot at and almost killed by the Brotherhood a few moments ago, just outside."

She paused, scanning the room and hoping to catch the eye of a Brotherhood member who might be in the crowd. "It is sickening to see how far White supremacy will go with its stupidity. I need every Brotherhood member in here today, acting like a summit participant, to hear me and hear me well. You have already lost. Your strategy and tactics are only working against you. Your power is diminished and your antiquated ideologies no longer have enough relevance to be taken seriously. Not only have we increased security presence this afternoon, but we have brought in a team of highly trained, ex-Special Forces members and planted them in our numbers this afternoon. They are trained to sniff out your stench and make you feel the consequences, should it come to that," Pamela finished.

It was quiet enough to hear a pin drop in the banquet room. Pamela knew the power of words. She also knew the power of being able to back those words up with action. Given her high profile in the community, and in the nation, she was able to rub shoulders with many high-level people, some of whom included the ex-Special forces members she spoke about. She could call them at a moment's notice if ever she needed help. When the Brotherhood and other terrorist groups had made appearances at some of her previous events, she'd learned she needed to be ready for armed self-defense and resistance should it come to that.

"Now that we've got that out the way, back to our scheduled program, ya'll," she said with her magnetic charm. The summit attendees clapped and shouted. "We have to let these people know we will not be intimidated, nor distracted, from our mission. As long as we stay the course, we will fulfill it. I encourage all of you here today, lean in even more to this work. The Brotherhood's presence confirms we are getting closer to what we are after. And they are scared. We will continue to apply the pressure until we break this demon of systemic racism in the U.S." Pamela said, raising her voice.

The crowd cheered and clapped again. Someone shouted to Pamela, "You are a badass, Pamela, we love you!"

"You know I love y'all, too. I'm so proud of this community. We will prevail. I want everyone to enjoy their lunch. We have an exciting segment next a big surprise.

For the last couple of years, I've been trying to figure out ways to cleverly make talking about race and racial difference easier and more common. Workshops and other forms of training are great and have their place, but I wanted to develop something that could get into the collective consciousness. And then it hit me, we North Americans love our entertainment. So what better way of practicing conversations about race that lead to systemic change than through playing a board game?

My team and I got together and created *Addressing the Elephant in the Room*, a game with a low barrier to entry for people seeking to have conversations surrounding race," Pamela said with great excitement.

"That's dope, why didn't I think of that?" someone shouted. Everyone, including Pamela, laughed.

"Thank you. Just know the name is trademarked," Pamela said. Again, everyone laughed.

"We thought that a great way to test the game as we prepare it for the market would be to have each table group play a couple rounds. After lunch, you will have an opportunity to play a beta version of the game. So eat up! And get ready to have some fun as we also deepen our learning," Pamela concluded.

PLAYING THE GAME

I hope you all enjoyed your lunch. It's time to move into what may prove to be one of the highlights of this year's summit. We are going to play the *Addressing the Elephant in the Room Board Game*.

This is the beta version, so I'm sure there are still a few kinks to work out. Our hope is that you enjoy playing the game and also provide us with valuable feedback about how to make the game better before it goes to market. Now, before we bring the game out, I'd like to explain the rules and purpose of this exercise." Pamela looked behind her at a PowerPoint presentation waiting on the screen.

The gameboard is designed to look like a pyramid, to mirror U.S. economic and social structures. The top of the pyramid represents liberation. When I say liberation, I mean the state of being able to live as one's true self without fear of consequences. Since the game is centered around race, we're keeping our definition of liberation focused on that. A player wins the game when they climb to the top of the pyramid, reaching liberation. We want the game to be a tool to help those who play it have effective conversations about race, racial differences, and racism. Most importantly, we hope those conversations lead to significant systemic change. Everybody got that?"

Pamela saw folks nodding throughout the crowd, so she kept going. "Now let's get into a few important aspects of gameplay. There are five different sets of cards used in the game. One set of profile cards and four sets of game cards. Before starting the game, every player will select a profile card at random. Your profile card will determine your racial social status, net worth, and education level within the game – all key factors in how people are treated in real life. Some of you may have high racial social status in real life, but in the game, the reverse may be true. Just like in real life, you must pick your profile cards randomly because we don't get to choose our race or ethnicity when we are born. Each profile consists of racial social status, net worth, and education level. We chose these aspects because often, these are the main determinants of success in the U.S. Of course, there are many more that could've been added, but we feel these are at the core of social status in our society.

To start the game, the players must decide, as a group, which player will go first. If there is no agreement about who goes first, the person who draws a profile card with the highest social status gets to decide. Much like in real society, those who have a certain skin color dictate which opportunities and rewards go to whom. You all see the pattern here, right? If multiple people have the same racial social status in the game, the player with the highest net worth gets to decide who goes first. If there is still a tie, choose the person with the highest education level on their Profile Card.

Let's move on to the game cards. There are four sets of cards: Solution Cards, Awareness Cards, Conflict Cards, and Moment of Equity Cards. When you roll the dice, the color you roll will indicate which type of card you will pick-up. The type of card you pick-up will determine how many spaces up or down you move on your ladder. Although the object of the game is to get to the liberation point at the top of the pyramid, the most important aspect of the game is the conversations you engage in along the way. For example, let's say a player rolls the dice and is directed to pick up a Solution Card. The player will read the card aloud, then other players will take turns discussing the situation and presenting a possible solution. The player who drew the card will then move up or down on their ladder, depending on what the card dictates. Here's an example of how a Solution Card might read:

Mass Incarceration has plagued the Black community in the U.S. for centuries. Discuss three ways mass incarceration can be eradicated in the U.S.

We believe conversations about topics like this can be the gateway to real-life liberation. Conversations can change our thoughts, our thoughts influence our actions, our actions become habits, and our habits influence systems. And that is how systemic change comes about.

We purposely didn't set a time limit for how long these conversations can go. But you are allowed to use a timer if you want gameplay to move faster. We leave that for you to decide. I might sound like a broken record, but I must reiterate that the object of the game is to engage in effective conversations. Getting to the top of the pyramid only acts as something to aim for in that particular moment. Better yet, let's say it represents *closure*.

Now, let's say you roll the dice and then need to pick up a Conflict Card. Conflict Cards present clear disagreement without clear solutions. One example of a Conflict Card is:

You and your long-term friend have a strong disagreement about which presidential candidate to support. You feel one candidate is overtly racist, but your friend supports that candidate regardless. How might this disagreement impact your friendship?

I also want to add that there are Positive Conflict Cards, which present solution-oriented conflicts. Here's an example:

You and one of your work colleagues frequently butt heads because you communicate differently based on your different cultural upbringing (which are directly tied to your racial background). What is one strategy you can employ to stop having so many conflicts with your colleagues?

Again, after a question is posed, players spend time discussing it and then proceed up the ladder according to the number of rungs the card indicates. You can move up or down with Conflict Cards because we, the gamemakers, wanted to make sure we conveyed that conflict can be an extremely healthy and necessary element in liberation. Additionally, the reality is that arguments and conflict-driven conversations take place across racial differences, and sometimes, common ground just can't be found because the parties engaged are unwilling to lower their guard to reach mutual understanding. But we believe this tension is a necessary ingredient for growth. Therefore, the game rewards players for taking opportunities to engage in healthy conflict via conversation.

Okay, on to Awareness Cards. An Awareness Card simply relays information, although very important information. These cards highlight specific moments in history, statistics, or facts that will help players grow in their understanding of racial equity. Awareness Cards don't permit players to move up or down the ladder, because in real life, awareness without action is pointless. Awareness, when coupled with enforced policies, has teeth.

Awareness Cards should inform your responses to questions posed on other cards. For example, there is an Awareness Card that presents facts about the practice of redlining, or the denial of a loan or insurance to someone because they live in an area deemed too poor. The information from this card can inform a player's response to a Solution or Conflict Card. This helps conversations maintain some objectivity and basis of fact and truth.

The game also has Moment of Equity cards. These cards present achieved racial equity. For example:

An association of realtors create and implement a program designed to provide Black homebuyers with significant down payment assistance, to address decades of redlining and predatory lending aimed at Black people in the U.S.

If it isn't apparent yet, we want this game to translate into practical application beyond its play. We also hope it inspires further study and investigation into topics discussed. As you play the game, we encourage you to keep your elephant stress balls handy, as you may need them when conversations get intense. Just know that intensity is part of the game and having conversations about race in general. Even those of us well-versed in having conversations about race have moments when we need to be challenged to think deeper about why we believe what we do. As long as we actively seek to make our society better for people of all racial identities, we are headed in the right direction. Okay, how about we get started playing the game?"

At that moment, several summit staffers entered the room pushing carts filled with *Addressing the Elephant in the Room* board games. They went to each table and put a game box right in the middle. There was a lot of chatter and curiosity about the game and the conference room filled with noise.

Some of the summit attendees began removing the shrink-wrapping from the games while others watched. Everyone was ready to play. Some participants fidgeted in their seats, not knowing what to expect. There were no facilitators, only the participants having *real* conversations about race that could lead to *real* conflict.

"Let's get ready to rumbllllllle" said Akash, an Indian man, as he opened the game box at his table. A few of his tablemates chuckled. His table was made up of a young White man named Brent who was in his thirties, a Pacific Islander woman named Heirani who looked a bit older, and a young Black woman named Tasha who couldn't have been more than twenty-five.

As he opened the box, Brent reached in and started pulling out game pieces and cards. He passed them around so others in the group would get a chance to look at them. The game had vibrant colors and a beautiful, simple design that rivaled those of the most popular games. "This is going to be good," Heirani said to herself, still loud enough for the group to hear.

"Mmmmhmmm," Tasha said in agreement as she looked at some of the game cards. She read one aloud:

Conflict Card
You are walking through a luxury department store and you notice you are being watched like a hawk. You believe it's due to your racial background. How do you respond and what are you hoping will result from your actions?
Move down the social ladder 2 rungs.

"It will be interesting to hear how you all would respond to this. I've experienced this on more than a few occasions." Tasha said.

"Let's pull our profile cards so we can determine who goes first," Akash said. He could tell Brent didn't like how he'd taken the lead and was trying not to let his irritation show. He understood that White men are taught at a young age how to mask their true emotions.

"I'll go ahead and shuffle them," said Brent. He shuffled the cards, then passed Profile Cards, face down, to each person. "Okay, moment of truth. I'll read mine first."

When he flipped the card over, disappointment was advertised across his face. "Education level: GED. Net worth: $10k or less. My racial social status is low, too. This isn't right," he said with a pout on his face.

"You realize this is just a game, right?" retorted Heirani. "Is your White privilege really that fragile?"

Brent fired back. "I'm just trying to understand the game. There's plenty of people who have GED's that are worth well above $10k. It doesn't seem right that the game pigeonholes them."

Wanting to de-escalate things, Akash jumped in. "How about we just reshuffle the cards and try again?"

In a knee-jerk reaction, Tasha said, "Uh-uh, we need to play the cards we have been dealt. That's how it is in real life, right?" She turned her card over and read it out loud.

She laughed loudly. "Ain't that something. I got a PhD and I am paid two milli, baby!" She and the Pacific Islander Woman high-fived.

"We'll *definitely* keep these cards, okaaay," Tasha said.

"Whatever," Brent responded under his breath.

"So it looks like you're clearly going first," Akash said to Tasha.

"It appears that way," Tasha responded, ready to dig into the game.

Heirani and Akash both had profile cards with middle-class elements.

Brent, still visibly upset about the card he was dealt, handed Tasha the dice. One had numbers on it and the other only had colors: red, black, and white. She took them without hesitation and ignored his frustration. She had experience moving past White discomfort to get to where she needed to go. She rolled the dice and landed on a C, for conflict . She checked the rules. She had to pull a Conversation Card and move up 3 spaces. She moved up the pyramid's ladder three rungs and grabbed the appropriate Conversation Card. It was a *Positive Conflict Card.*

You and a colleague frequently butt heads because your communication styles are different. Communication styles are shaped by cultural upbringing, which is directly tied to racial background. What is one strategy you can employ to minimize conflict between yourself and your colleague?

She read the card aloud and followed up with, "ouch," to the group. She sighed like she was bracing herself for the full weight of the incoming responses. She expected to hear things she didn't like from the other players.

Heirani responded first. "Let me say this before we discuss this question: I don't like it. The question makes race sound more like a biological construct than a social one. I mean, why is it assumed that cultural upbringing is tied to racial background? Does anyone else not see the issue with this question?"

"Well obviously there are aspects of race that influence how we grew up right?" said Tasha. "For example, I grew up in a pretty affluent neighborhood, but my younger brother was still cautioned as a teenager to be very careful around police. 'Don't give them any reason to shoot you because they'll easily use it,' is what my parents would say. That in and of itself shaped the way my brother and I viewed police. Police were people to fear, as opposed to people we associate with positivity or safety.

I'm old enough to remember the Rodney King beating, and the subsequent trial in which none of the officers who were caught on tape beating him were convicted. So, even though NWA was before my time, when I heard their song, "Fuck the Police," I found myself in agreement with it. I'm not saying it was the right attitude to have, but it was justified by the paranoia I saw my brother carry about the police, my own negative experiences, and what I've witnessed happening to other Black people when faced with law enforcement. Little has changed in how Black Americans are treated by law enforcement, from its inception during slavery to now. There is hardly any accountability for their abuse or murder by police.

In the workplace, I've had co-workers tell me I'm overreacting when I've made comments about headlines of yet another Black American being murdered by police. It's gotten to the point now that I don't even bring it up because I know no one will understand, or care to understand, my point of view."

"I'm sorry you have to go through that," said Akash. "I can imagine it feels like psychological safety is non-existent in your workplace. Although the social context is different for me, I can relate to being treated as less-than-human because of the caste system I was born into. Here in the U.S., I've come to learn that race operates as its own caste system and promotes the advancement of some and the degradation of others."

Tasha nodded her head in agreement. "Yep, I rarely feel safe to express my point of view at work. I don't even feel at liberty to be my authentic self much of the time. Now, I'm beginning to care less and less about what other people think about me, or how I'm perceived. I need to care for my mental health, instead. Having to put on a mask and change my tone so I can be accepted at work, or elsewhere, is so draining."

After she said this, everyone at the table remained quiet for a short while, processing the weight of what she'd shared. After a minute or two, the silence turned to awkwardness. Tasha chimed in, "Let's discuss strategy. Have any of you employed any effective strategies that led to conflict resolution when cultural upbringing was a key factor?"

Heirani spoke up. "I have found that not judging someone for where they are in their thinking, and instead trying to get an understanding of what led them to that point, goes a long way. This is not an easy practice and there's still a chance a relationship can turn sour even with this understanding in place. But for the most part, opening myself up to hear other peoples' stories helps me find commonality. Once I find that, I build on it."

Brent, who had remained mostly silent since his earlier conflict, commented, "I like that approach. I think considering someone's intent is important when conflict due to racial or cultural difference arises. I think professional relationships could be a lot stronger if people focused more on intent. I mean, I never intend to offend anyone, but that's usually not what's focused on if I do offend them. I get written off as another racist, privileged, White guy when I make a mistake with a person of color. "

"I'm actually glad you brought that up," Heirani said. "Intent vs. impact is not highlighted as much as it should be. However, I disagree with you about the importance of focusing more on intent. Impact is what really matters. Think of it like this, let's say I'm driving and I'm minding my own business, enjoying the ride. I accidentally run a red light and you are crossing the street and *boom*! I hit you with my car, severely injuring you. Now, it wasn't my *intention* to hurt you, but nonetheless, you have to go to the hospital immediately because of my actions. And I would be responsible for your injuries. Rightly so. Should I not be held accountable?"

Brent took a few seconds to think before he responded. He saw the logic in her question. "I get where you're trying to go with this. Yes, I feel there should be a level of accountability for the driver. But there also must be some accountability on the part of the pedestrian. Were they jaywalking? Were they paying attention to oncoming traffic? What time of day was it when they got hit and were they wearing clothing that made them visible? The accountability you're talking about goes both ways, right?"

Tasha interjected, "Your argument sounds like the centuries-old loophole used to justify the dehumanization of Black people. We've been enslaved, raped, murdered, stolen, robbed, and incarcerated, yet the burden of proof is always on us. The system that continues to commit these acts against us never looks itself in the mirror, it seeks to point out why we are deserving of such treatment. Your comments are an echo of the racist matrix created by your forefathers."

Brent defended himself, "Whoa, whoa, whoa! Hold on there. It's unfair that you place me in the same boat as racists. I'm an individual. I think and act of my own accord. I also feel like you clearly misunderstood what I said. You've made up your mind about me and have already put me into a box. I wasn't saying the person responsible for hitting the pedestrian shouldn't be accountable, I said accountability goes both ways. What has happened to Black People in America is utterly shameful. So shameful that I sometimes find myself embarrassed to be White. However, that doesn't take away from the fact that the Black community has a responsibility to itself."

Sensing he had just entered deep water he most likely wasn't equipped to swim in, the Black woman asked, "What responsibility does the Black Community have unto itself? Do tell."

"For starters, Black-on-Black killings and crime rates must be accounted for. There is so much focus placed on police shootings, but hardly any attention given to how those within your community harm each other. Also, when I listen to rap music, I hear nothing but how a Black man will kill another Black man and not in those words, either. They talk about selling drugs to their community and how far they'd be willing to go to disrespect the opposite sex if it meant gaining the upper hand."

"What you are failing to see is that much of what you just mentioned stems from the White racist system we find ourselves in. Although many in the Black community do not subscribe to attitudes and opinions found in the rap music you've heard, that same music is popularized and pushed by major music companies with a vested interest in the continued mass incarceration of Black men and women. That type of rap music is what sells because rich White men do what's in their power to make it so. Have you ever wondered why this type of rhetoric is mainly heard in rap and hip – hop music? Don't you think White people and other racial groups have just as much dysfunction within their communities as ours? My guess is you probably don't think about that. But the truth is, the racist matrix, the interlocking web of systems created by Western European colonizers, has been designed to vilify Black people and make White people and others who identify as White look and feel superior. The designers of this matrix will always make it look like those who are stuck in it are the ones at fault. That's how this game keeps going. I'll tell you this though, many people are starting to wake up and see the matrix for what it is, including White people.

And more and more of those from your community are becoming sick of their own shit," Tasha finished.

"How do you expect anyone to take you and your cause seriously when you speak to people the way you do?" said Brent, his face turning red from anger. "I really hate to say this, I probably shouldn't, but there's a name for women who act like you are right now."

Tasha, with all the poise of a royal dignitary, replied, "Oh really, and what might that name be?"

"Well, they'd say, umm, they'd call you an angry Black woman, okay!" Brent shouted in a higher pitch than his normal tone. The table went dead silent. Akash and Heirani looked at each other in shock, not believing what Brent had just said. Still keeping her queen-like composure, Tasha responded without raising her voice.

"You're the one who is yelling and turning red, so who is the angry one? This is a teachable moment right here. In this nation, White anger, no matter how violent and brutal, is tolerated. Meanwhile, Black anger, no matter how justified, is labeled criminal and unacceptable. You know, I'm not even mad at you for what you just said. I could be, but I realize that what you're saying is just the White supremacist system speaking through you and you don't even realize it. In your mind, you're probably like, *how dare a Black woman speak to me this way*. You'll never admit it, and perhaps you don't even know you're thinking or feeling that way because those feelings and thoughts rage in a deeper part of you than you are ready to acknowledge.

"You've been conditioned to believe you are better than me, even though that is a complete and utter fallacy. It's a fallacy, boo boo. You are looking at a liberated Black woman who knows her value and the gift she is to the world. You can call me angry, but I know I am passionate about helping Black people break free from this system of White supremacy in this country. THIS COUNTRY!" She pointed at the ground with both hands.

A few people from surrounding tables looked up from their games to tune into the commotion. They went back to their discussions after a few moments. Pamela and her team had done a lot of preliminary work to normalize conflict surrounding conversations about race at the summit.

Somewhat at a loss for words, Brent said, "you know I don't fully agree with everything you said, but I'm willing to look at my own perspective and see where I, as a White man, have been getting it wrong. The last thing I want to do is invalidate your experience by speaking from a place of deep-rooted bias I'm probably not even aware of. The truth is, you've had to live under a weight I never lived under, and never will. I'm sorry I mislabeled you as an angry Black woman. Anger is totally justified due to what your community has experienced at the hand of my ancestors. Although I didn't create this system, which continues to work against you and your community, I want to do my part to dismantle it. Not that I or any White person is deserving of it, but I hope you will extend grace to me as I do the work necessary to learn how to be an anti-racist and become part of the solution to end systemic racism. I want to thank you for challenging me to grow."

Tasha was filled with a variety of emotions as she heard his thoughtful response. She was tired of extending grace to White people. She felt like Black people had been giving White people grace for centuries while Black people continued to suffer, be held down, and die from White apathy. But she kept her poker face on. She was all too familiar with the empty promises of well-meaning White folks. She knew that in moments like this, they make commitments they soon forget about, despite their epiphanies. Still, she held hope that maybe, just maybe, this man would make good on his words. "I'm not looking for any White person to save me or the Black community. We've proven we can survive and rise above the most adversarial circumstances. But I do sometimes wonder how much further we could go if those who created and benefit from a White supremacist system took a leading role in dismantling it. Perhaps wishful thinking on my part, but nonetheless, a girl can dream. As I extend this requested grace to you, I also need something in return."

"Name it," Brent said.

"I need you to get active *now*. Your learning must immediately be converted into action. And you must commit to staying action-oriented for the long haul, otherwise, this moment of clarity will not matter."

"Well, I don't know if this was the intended impact of the game, but I'll say I like the direction we're moving in," said Akash. The others nodded their heads in agreement.

"I still don't think we've addressed how we can reduce conflicts when a racial or cultural difference is at play," said Brent.

"I think the exchange you two just had addressed it perfectly," said Heirani.

"Really? How so?" said Tasha.

"I think it became evident through your exchange that some conflict is necessary, if not inevitable, if you want to arrive at a real solution. 'Going along to get along' can only take us so far in dialogues about race, and it doesn't take us far enough. You both demonstrated the importance of hearing the other side of the story, even if you don't agree with someone's opinion. And from there, one or both of you had to be willing to look at your own perspective and acknowledge beliefs you need to reevaluate. Coming from that place, our conflict can become healthy and productive. I think conflict can be productive when it leads to action, and then consistent action. Once action is consistent, it yields fruit in a relationship, at which point the conflict surrounding cultural upbringing will lessen. The only thing is, you can't decide when the action will yield fruit. It must happen organically. You can do everything in your power to speed that growth, but you cannot force it, especially if there was no fruit to begin with. What do you think?" Heirani sat back in her chair and looked at Akash.

"I agree with your points," said Akash. "I think the most important component in solving conflicts like this is a commitment to affirming what you do know, acknowledging what you don't, and taking-in the good from the other person involved, even if you don't like their delivery. And sometimes, getting a delivery you don't like is the thing you need to move in the right direction. There also has to come a point when you stop caring so much about someone's opinion and more about the *actual* person you are in a conflict with. It's almost like you have to have a conversation with yourself, first, and affirm that you want what's best for them even if you are at odds about a particular thing. I know this is easier said than done, but it is absolutely possible," Akash finished.

"Imagine that, the ability to care about other humans more than our opinions. Now that's a concept!" Brent said.

"Yep, if only it was easy to do," said Tasha. I find that many people are more committed to their opinions or causes than they are to human life. And all too often, people dig their heels into their opinions against Black people if there is even a semblance of progress economically, socially, or politically for us. One of the questions I hope this game will help us address is how we handle conflict stemming from racial differences when race, as a social construct, was created to dehumanize certain groups of people for the benefit of another, especially since this conflict is built into the bedrock of our nation?

"That's the question I'm most interested in answering. Interpersonal questions like the one we just discussed are good, but I feel the question I'm asking addresses the systemic root of racial inequity, which produces those types of interpersonal conflicts we're discussing, in the first place. But I digress."

"Great point," said Brent.

Again, a long silence hung over the table. Tasha broke that silence, yet again. "I wonder if this was the purpose of the game, to engage in dialogue much deeper than what the game cards suggest? I mean, we are literally still on the first question. We probably could've been on our fourth or fifth by now."

Heirani backed her up. "Whether we should be farther along or not, I think this has been time well spent. Our collective culture is always in such a rush that we don't take the time to really process things. But we can't rush through conversations about race and come up with an adequate solution. We've been steeped in this mess for centuries and it's going to take a lot more than a fireside chat or town hall meeting to dismantle it."

Akash chimed in. "So what would you say to someone who uses that perspective to drag their feet on dismantling racism?"

"Good question," replied Heirani. "The system of White supremacy thrives on foot dragging, or looking at the issue of racial divide as something so insurmountable that there is little to be done about it, if anything at all. My response to that is although American racism is so deeply embedded in our culture that it will take massive lifts to demolish it, we all must get our jack hammers and hard hats on and get to work. The areas of White supremacy we demolish today will make life much better for the next generation as they continue the work of creating a more equitable world. If we don't relent, we will see breakthroughs sooner than we think. We are living in a time of immense opportunity to make drastic changes to our society. I believe we have the power to greatly cripple racism within one generation and put a new foundation in place that kills it completely."

"Okay everyone, five more minutes until we wrap this portion of the summit up," Pamela announced from the podium.

"Shoot, has it been an hour already?" the White man said. "I can't believe one question took this much time. I was hoping to get deeper into the game."

"I think it was time well spent though," said the Black woman. "I don't think the object of the game is to necessarily win it as much as it is to have dialogue like we just did."

"I get that, but there are so many other topics for us to explore that we won't get a chance to," Brent responded.

"Well, how about we exchange contact information and perhaps we can get back together after the summit and play? I'm willing to host it at my place if that sounds good to everyone," Tasha said. Everyone nodded their heads in agreement.

"Okay, okay! Lets reconvene everyone. Let's talk about what you learned while playing the game, and also what you liked and what could be improved upon. We want to make sure the game experience conveys as much value as it possibly can before we take it to market. We've got mic runners, so please raise your hand if you have a comment and we'll get a mic over to you." Pamela said.

Several hands went up as Pamela looked over the audience. "Yes, the gentleman with the light blue sportcoat in the far back," she said. The mic runner dashed off to hand the mic to a gracefully aging Latino man so he could ask his question.

"Thanks Pamela, and thanks to your team for hosting this incredible event. My question is, are there guiding principles we should've had in mind while having these conversations in the game? It sort of felt like the Wild West while we played. I mean, people at our table were just going for it, myself included. There was a ton of productive conversation, but we stepped in shit a few times, too." The crowd laughed as he handed the mic back.

Pamela, laughing with the crowd, responded. "Great question. We intentionally did not provide guiding principles about how to have these conversations during the test run because we are still weighing the pros and cons of doing so. If you give people too much guidance, they may solely rely on that guidance and raw truth may not surface. However, this is something I'm still thinking about. Also, if you recall, we shared the RIGHTS Approach earlier in the day. Our hope was that you all could reference that approach while in conversation throughout the game. I see now that I should have highlighted that beforehand. Note to self for the next time. Let's take the next question from the woman in the back, with the yellow blouse."

The mic runner handed the mic to a Polynesian woman in a silk, canary-yellow blouse who appeared to be in her mid-thirties. "I want to second the gentleman who spoke before me in thanking you, Pamela, for creating space for us to come together to share our thoughts on race and learn from each other. I'd like to know, is the impact of this game solely to have conversations, or are there other outcomes we should expect? Thank you."

"Thank you for being here and bringing your energy and passion to this conversation, too," said Pamela. "In addition to hopefully making the conversation about race a little easier and normal to have, I'm hoping those playing the game can come up with strategies to eradicate systemic racism and spur equitable actions and systems. Conversations alone will not fix this massive issue, which is why we included Solution Cards. Solution Cards give players the opportunity to become more than game players. They can become a think tank! And hopefully, the strategies they come up with are ones they can take into the real world and apply.

"Another outcome I'd like to see is the comfortability of folks to work together across racial differences. You'll notice that the racial and ethnic makeup at your game tables is diverse. That was by design. The work of racial equity has the potential to unify us, especially if we share a common vernacular. I prefer you all go deeper than wider in your conversations during the game because you'll find that you can uncover a lot more by doing so. The questions in the game are mainly intented to be as prompts. Take the conversations where you want to go as long as they lead to action. Does this make sense?"

The Polynesian woman nodded her head yes.

"Ok great. Now, we have quite a few more hands raised, so let's get to as many folks as we can before our keynote speaker," said Pamela.

Derek shuffled in his seat when he heard Pamela bring up the keynote. So much had happened to him since the beginning of the summit that he wasn't sure if he wanted to share his keynote address as it currently was. He recounted the way he had been insulted by the hotel concierge when he first got to the hotel; the argument between Liz and the hotel staff person in which he intervened but hurt Liz in the process; and the most significant wounding he experienced that day of almost getting killed by the Brotherhood outside the hotel. Not to mention, he was still waiting to hear back from the CEO at Innovative Energy about his position. He felt the weight of the world on his shoulders and his current keynote address would not give him the release he needed from that weight. He decided he would still use some of the elements from his original speech, but for the most part, speak from the heart. He felt that was what the people needed right then, himself included.

THE KEYNOTE

The summit attendees were in a buzz as they returned to their seats after the fifteen-minute break. Many were continuing conversations they started during the game. Some were crying, hugging, or scowling from unresolved conflict. Pamela relished the sea of emotions and dispositions she saw as she looked over the audience. She knew disruption was taking place, and that was a good thing.

"Welcome back everybody. We are on the last leg of our summit today but we are ending strong. Our keynote speaker, Derek Blain, is a highly sought-after thought leader in the DEI space. He is the Global VP of Talent, Diversity, and Inclusion at Innovative Energy. In other words, the brotha is bad y'all..."

Derek sat near the stage, lost in thought as Pamela introduced him. Her words sounded muffled to him as he replayed various events of the day. He recalled the numerous murders of Black people by police officers that he'd witnessed on media over the years; driving his Tesla through the inner city and feeling survivor's remorse for being able to make a better life for himself; and realizations about how many kids who looked like him would not have the same opportunities he did. He was both thankful and mournful about being the anomaly, the outlier in most environments he found himself in. He thought about his Black peers, who had equal or greater qualifications than their White counterparts, but who continued to get looked over for promotions and advancements into senior executive positions because of entrenched racist cultures in workplaces. He thought about several of his cousins, a few of whom he felt were smarter than him, but who were incarcerated due to petty drug offenses. He had even contributed money toward hiring legal representation on their behalf during their trials and incarceration. He also remembered how he was often the only person with brown skin sitting at tables of power and influence. It all bothered him to his core. Even though he was grateful for the success he was able to garner over the years, he still felt the weight of the needs of his people, many of whom were not so fortunate. He reflected on the two different worlds he was a part of: one was clean, bright, and seemed to offer many opportunities; the other held joy but was often shrouded with constant assaults of death, dysfunction, and struggle. He entered both worlds everyday and he had to resist the urge to choose one over the other. He was meant to live in both.

These thoughts scurried through his mind and he got wrapped up in his own mental maze until he heard his name.

"...Derek Blain everyone! Please welcome him to the stage," Pamela said. The crowd cheered and applauded. He gathered himself and put on his professional mask. He stood up, walked to the podium, hugged Pamela, and then looked out at the sea of faces eager to hear his words. He took a deep breath that wasn't noticeable. The same technique he used with the Brotherhood moments ago, He practiced it religiously, especially when he felt nervous. But he had been through so much today that he knew he really didn't need it. He knew the right words would spill out of him with powerful effect because his emotions were so raw.

"Having the race conversation. Hmmm. Now ain't that a concept," Derek began. "We've come so far in our society in terms of technology, medicine, and energy. But when it comes to race, we seem to be stuck." Derek paused for a long while, wanting the audience to experience some discomfort from the delay. He waited even after he saw people beginning to fidget, pull out their phones, and open side conversations. Finally, he continued.

When I entered DEI work several years ago, I did it with the hopes of creating a better future for my children. Fifteen years later, that hope is still intact. However, I'm less naïve and have prepared my kids for a world that, in many ways, is still hostile to the color of their skin. There are so many things outside my control that I've now shifted my focus to modeling the type of resilience I pray they will develop when confronting ancient systems of oppression which merely change faces and mediums over time.

With that said, I chose to speak at this summit today because the race conversation is still of utmost importance for us to have together if we hope to get unstuck. It is in the exchange of ideas, stories, experiences, and perspectives that we can make more informed decisions. Although race is a social construct, it's quite clear that it is here to stay as a social reality. When so much of what is tangible in our world has been built on the idea of race, it is difficult to envision a future in which race can be left out of the picture. From my perspective, and within my culture, so much of our identity is welded to the idea of Blackness. It's ironic that this concept of Blackness was created to enslave and dehumanize us, but somehow, some way, we have been transforming that concept into something to empower and bring us together. It's ironic, but true, nonetheless. We have become adept at using the very thing meant to oppress us as a guiding light to our liberation. Some of you may disagree with that idea and argue that race, as a concept, should be done away with completely. I understand that perspective, but my gut tells me we would be leaving behind a repository of power and energy to heal the very wound racism has caused. Only time will tell.

But what's clear to me now is that we all owe it to ourselves to be honest about where we are at this very moment. I think the fallacy of living in a post-racial society has been thrown out the window recently. Many of us would agree with that. What we are still trying to figure out, though, is the depth of the wound that racism has caused, how we can collectively heal it, and what we should expect from one another in the process.

The most obvious and visible wounds are the legacy of generational poverty, slave labor, or should I say mass incarceration, underrepresentation in the work environment, health and wellbeing disparities, and government sanctioned brutality against communities of color, specifically Black Americans. We've now entered into a time in our history where these atrocities are part of our collective consciousness. And while I am glad they are now being highlighted, I feel we are in a strange place in which we are celebrating the fact that our – Black America's – trauma is simply being recognized. Don't get me wrong, I get it. When you haven't been heard for so long, or acknowledged, that recognition can feel like oxygen. But this celebration is akin to a victim of sexual abuse relishing in seeing the children and benefactors of their abusers, and those who perpetuate the system in which this type of abuse happens, simply publicly acknowledging that abuse happened and is continuing to happen." Derek paused to let the weight of what he said sink in.

Again, don't get me wrong, celebration can be an important part of healing. It marks the progress one has crossed in life. But we can't get stuck there, not when the system of racist oppression is still intact. One could even beg the question, can we ever fully dismantle this system, especially when it is tied to every institution of our nation?

And the anti-racist institutions we see now have been created as a result of what? Racism! The boom in the DEI space is the result of what? Racism. There is even racism inside these so-called DEI practices. I am not implying DEI practitioners are bad people. I am saying this slime, this ooze, this cancer we call racism is so hard-boiled into the fabric of our nation that we have yet to get a firm understanding of how ubiquitous it is.

Now, I'm an eternal optimist. I'm not quite sure how I became this way, but I believe systemic racism can be completely eradicated. This belief is balanced with pragmatism. I've seen waves of promising solutions come and go . Those solutions have not been sustained. And I don't think individual racism will ever be done away with. That has to do with people's individual choices. But *systemic racism* can be completely dismantled because it has to do with objective components such as policy, business, and economics. Aspects of these fields can be measured and changed methodically. This isn't to say the hearts and minds of individual people who occupy these fields do not need to be engaged and hopefully changed, it's saying changes in policy, business, and economics will give people both the *incentive* and *imperative* to change. There is a strong reason to evolve when that evolution is tied to our paychecks, networks, and influence. As a society, we've proven we can't make racial equity a sustained priority with good intentions alone. We must build structure around those good intentions which can be perpetuated and carried over to following generations.

While the need and crying-out for racial equity is several centuries old, the pathways which we are taking to get there are very new. These pathways haven't been around long enough for us to determine if they are truly effective. But what we can determine, what we know, is that consistency yields fruit over time. And once we see that fruit, we must double-down on our efforts. I'm not suggesting we wait to see fruit before we start making additional investments into the work. That would be a mistake. We need to act now, especially because it will take everything we have to collectively slay this ancient monster who mutates and transfigures itself over generations. There are parts of this monster that are archaic, and it still employs methods of terrorism and intimidation to try to impose its will." Derek paused. He chose his words carefully before he spoke again.

I wasn't going to share this, but ... uhhh ... we are in a time where we must speak our truth. I learned that today, from you, Liz," Derek looked directly at Liz, seated a few tables away from the stage. "It's funny, we are here having a conversation about race meant to advance racial equity, but I was still treated like a second class citizen the moment I walked through the doors of this hotel. I'm not trying to put the hotel on blast, I've actually stayed here many times, but I, the keynote speaker, had to jump through hoops to be granted permission to come into the conference space. All the while, I watched an older White man, who was also checking in at the conference, receive the royal treatment while I was psychologically patted down. For God's sake, my damn picture and name was posted all throughout this venue and that still wasn't enough for the concierge to treat me like I belonged here. I'm bringing this up because systems that perpetuate this kind of racist treatment are all around us, in establishments, organizations, and institutions we know and love. Light-touch assaults like this accumulate and create a clear path for more serious ones. Every small act of dehumanization makes it easier to take Black life without blinking an eye. These consistent acts normalize the mistreatment of Black bodies, minds, and spirits.

I don't have to look far to find an example to prove my point."

Derek took a moment to regain his composure. He stepped back from the podium as his emotions got the best of him. With a quiver in his voice and holding back tears, he returned to the podium.

The Brotherhood pulled guns on me today and almost murdered me just outside the doors of this conference room." A small tear rolled down his cheek. Derek wiped it away before anyone could notice. He wasn't a crier or an overly emotional person, but what he felt was seeping through him and bubbling to the surface.

Now look, I aint trying to play victim here. That's not how I was raised. I'm telling you this to expose where our so-called *progressive* nation is truly at. I'm not saying anything many of you don't know already, but I am putting a face and name to it to make it extremely relevant. I, Derek Blain, Global Vice President of Diversity, Equity, and Inclusion at Innovative Energy, was almost gunned down by the Brotherhood right outside of the Having the Race Conversation Summit, where I am serving as the keynote speaker. Let that sink in."

The room was silent enough to hear a pin drop. The ringer on someone's phone went off, but the sound wasn't enough to distract a single person in the audience of hundreds of people. The audience was captivated by Derek's words. He was already a powerful and effective communicator, but his lived experience created an even deeper connection with the listeners in the audience.

What's more, there wasn't a single police officer in sight who tried to intervene. When one did show up, he acted as if he was in support of what the Brotherhood was doing. I got more support from the crowd witnessing the event than from local law enforcement.

I could easily have been another hashtag trending on social media tonight. And more than likely, my family and those who know me wouldn't have even been able to grieve. They probably would have been forced to use their energy to protect my character. All too often, when a Black person gets killed by White supremacy, the first question asked is, what did he do to deserve it? It's the same, old, and tired play from the same, old, White supremacist playbook. These neo lynchings go unchecked and unpunished, creating even more psychological damage to Black people and emboldening the monster. The fact that the man who murdered 17 year old Trayvon Martin, George Zimmerman, is still a free man still perplexes me to my core. I won't get into that though.

Black folks are often told to wait for justice. The thing is, when you are Black, dead Black bodies must heap up to the heavens before this so-called *justice* comes our way. And that only comes after we have marched, protested, boycotted, posted, sued, occupied, been tear gassed, been shot with rubber bullets, and imprisoned. These moments of *justice* don't come for free or because it's the right thing to do. We have to manually push justice along.

This begs the question, where does the power to change things lie? You probably have your own ideas about the answer to this question, but I am convinced that the power lies with us, the people. These systems will only go as far as we push them, especially for Black and historically disenfranchised people of color. There is absolutely no system within the White supremacist framework that works on our behalf. And this is not by mistake. This system, this real life matrix, was socially engineered to operate this way from the very beginning. It's doing what it was made to do.

And while we see overt parts of this system – the Brotherhood, as an example – overt racism is dying out. It may continue to exist in some pockets, but ultimately, its time has ended. The real fight is against the insidious, covert parts of the system, those undercover policies and languages cloaked with an aura of *wokeness*. This is the part of the monster that is hardest to detect.

The monster is designed to hold and wield absolute power at all costs. There is no negotiating with it, and it does not tolerate anything threatening its power. Like I said earlier, people have the right to feel how they want to feel on a personal level, but the system, the monster, is what must be dealt with if we hope to achieve sustained liberation.

I don't know about you all, but I am tired of having only moments of justice. Justice needs to be an expected outcome every time we seek it, and we should be able to gain it without the need for organized protests and civil unrest.

What I'm going to say next will get me into trouble, but at this point, I don't care. A change occurred in me today when I was laying on the ground, after almost getting my head blown off. I realized I'm only wasting air if I don't do my part to slay the monster. For many of us in this room, this is a life-or-death struggle. When abuse, murder, and slander are excused with no consequences, genocide becomes the natural progression. Even at the most visible levels, law enforcement and the criminal justice system have worked together to protect White people who kill Black people. Period. This is part of the elephant in the room that we all see, right? The cop who came to the scene after I was shot at willingly overlooked the shooting, even after various people screamed-out what had happened to me! And what's worse is that taxpayers end up footing the bill for police misconduct. Civil justice isn't my area of expertise, so I'll point out a few ways the elephant shows up in my domain: corporate America.

The White supremacist paradigm in corporate workplaces is killing Black people in the same ways crooked cops are, just not with bullets. Firm evidence has shown that racism is a leading cause of fatal health problems in Black people and people of color. Virtually all large U.S. Firms are controlled by White people who hold the highest positions of power. Executive teams in our largest companies and organizations need to look more like us, people of color, rather than simply including one or two token people of color. Even tokenized people of color are few and far between on leadership teams and boards. What's more, these tokenized people are not empowered to help shape the workplace culture or give more opportunities to others who look like them. I've heard, in a variety of ways, the sentiment of, *'you just need to be grateful that you are here.'*

The few Black leaders who somehow, by the grace of God, maneuver to the top of these organizations, are under immense pressure. Often, they are called a sellout by their own community because they rose despite incredible odds stacked against them. Yet, despite rising up through the ranks, the monster is always seeking ways to make them a puppet or undermine them. They are under constant pressure to deliver and often lack the support needed from the CEO or Board of directors. On top of that, they can still be shot dead in the street by law enforcement or a zealous White citizen if they aren't in their corporate uniform.

The rabbit hole of systemic racism is so deep in this country that there will never be a single solution for ferreting it out. That's what many of us have been hoping and looking for, even though there isn't one. The solution lies in a combination of various strategies that must be sustained and expanded upon over several generations. Essentially, we as DEI professionals, need to focus on working ourselves out of a job. We will have made progress when our offices for racial equity are unnecessary.

Let me break down a critical element that must be present in order to end systemic racism. In a capitalistic society, we must always start with the money and the money makers. They have the most influence. Should corporate America ever decide to get onboard the racial equity train, we will begin to see things change in our nation. Once CEOs of Fortune 500 companies demand that their organizations become racially equitable, the monster will be in its final days. What does a racially equitable corporate America look like?

It looks like a Board of Directors made up of at least fifty percent Black and other people of color. At the very least, racial representation in the C-Suite and on a board must be commensurate with the demographics of the country or state the firm is headquartered in. Those in leadership positions at the firm must have a hypersensitive focus on the company's culture, ensuring all talent in the organization has a positive experience at work. As this landscape is established, the company must put systems in place to ensure the mid-level management and above hold a significant number of Black people and other people of color. Because companies engaged in a strong racial equity plan are great places for people of color to work at, word of mouth will spread and more people of color will join the firm, grow with the company, and advance into key leadership positions.

Firms which have traditionally withheld leadership roles from Black people and reserved them for White people will make sure they have effective mentorship and leadership tracts in place for emerging Black leaders and leaders from other historically marginalized racial groups. This is a radical idea, I know. But the detrimental effects of segregation haven't gone anywhere. They just show up differently now. Drinking fountains for Whites and 'colored' might be gone, but Black employees are still concentrated at the bottom, and White people are still concentrated at the top, of our professional organizations. This is the status quo, and a shameful truth all major companies in this country are only beginning to realize they must grapple with.

The question that organizations need to be asking daily is, *how do we replace oppressive systems with liberating ones?* A common deflection one might hear in response to this is, *we need to focus on the business and the bottom line.* To that point, I argue racial equity is directly linked to the bottom line. A recent Citi report entitled "Closing the Racial Wealth Gap" stated that systemic racism, particularly around the racial wealth gap, has cost the U.S. sixteen trillion dollars over the last twenty years. Let me put it to you in a way that contextualizes it further: Apple, Amazon, Microsoft, and Google have market caps of one trillion or more, respectively. That means systemic racism has suppressed the birth of sixteen more companies who could have been added to this list. Systemic racism hurts us, collectively, no matter someone's racial background. I know I'm preaching to the choir, so let me conclude with possible solutions. How does that sound?"

The audience responded without missing a beat. Several "Yeah's!" and "Go for it!" comments permeated the air.

"Cool, I wanted to make sure I wasn't losing anyone." Derek knew he had this audience in the palm of his hand. He was going to make the most of it.

That same study showed that we could add five trillion dollars to the U.S. GDP over the next five years if we close the racial wealth gap today. Closing the racial wealth gap has four key areas of concentration. They are housing, education, wages, and investment. I encourage each of you to reflect on the influence you wield, your organizations, and your personal network, and think through how you can utilize these to address these specific areas. Several studies have shown that owning one's home is one of the most rudimentary ways to build wealth in this country. Yet only forty percent of Black Americans own a home, whereas seventy-five percent of White Americans own theirs. And this is no accident. Both the real estate industry and our government have been complicit in racially discrimination when it comes to Black home-ownership. Financial institutions must be intentional about opening home financing opportunities to the Black community. Not only that, but they must be held accountable for the types of loans they offer to Black borrowers. Many Black people have not fully recovered from the 2007 financial crisis, when predatory subprime mortgages were being doled out to Black families like water.

So what can we do to change course and open more opportunities for Black Americans and other historically marginalized racial groups to build wealth through homeownership? The National Association of Realtors developed a five-year plan outlining how the real estate industry can do exactly that. For the sake of time, I won't get into the weeds of that plan, but the key areas of focus are:

First: building more homes to increase supply Second: building more homes in Opportunity Zones. Opportunity Zones are defined by *Forbes* as, 'economically distressed communities where new investments, under certain conditions, may be eligible for preferential tax treatment.' Third: increasing access to down payment assistance."Fourth: strengthening the FHA's loan program. And lastly: expanding alternative credit scoring models.

Next, let's talk about education, specifically, about closing the achievement gap. First, let me define the achievement gap. It is the disparity in academic performance between groups of students, including disparities in dropout rates, promotion rates, college admittance rates, standardized test scores, and advanced placement and honors course selection rates. Schools in predominantly Black areas are typically underfunded and have less experienced teachers. Yet, Black students and other students from marginalized racial backgrounds that attend majority-White schools often suffer academically due to the unwelcoming environments they are learning in. In other words, the culture of these schools does not foster positive academic experiences for them. Further, we must look at whether students from historically marginalized backgrounds are being encouraged to go to college, if they are exposed to advanced placement classes, and whether they are connected with internship opportunities. In most cases, these things happen disproportionately less for Black students than their White counterparts. Our education system perpetuates these inequities and causes the achievement gap to both widen and persist.

Now, let's talk about solutions. A case study of a school district in Texas provides us with some potential success factors we should consider. At the school district, principals and school administrators believed they could close the racial achievement gap and support their teachers' efforts at the same time. This belief gave teachers space to be creative, try new strategies, and go above and beyond their regular job duties to help Black students. This is called collective efficacy. It reminds me of a principle I learned reading a book called *You Are the Solution* by Philip Jacobs. The first chapter of the book is entitled "Believing You Are the Solution." In it, Philip affirms that effective solutions all start from a place of belief. We act in line with what we believe, and those beliefs stem from what we value. Between the belief that their school district could close the racial achievement gap and gain buy-in from key individuals, the teachers and school administrators made a radical change in partnership with Black students. And in good ol' Texas, of all places! No shade to anyone who is from Texas, by the way."

A few people in the audience laughed.

Onto wages. Wages tend to be a sticky and sore spot for a lot of organizations because of the legal and reputational ramifications if practices of dimiscration are discovered . But since we are addressing the elephant in the room, we gotta deal with it. On average, Black Americans earn thirty percent less than White Americans. When we break these numbers down by race and gender, the disparity is even worse. Black women earn only sixty two *cents* for every dollar White men earn. This discrepancy in income, when coupled with other structural inequities, makes it difficult for Black families to save, invest, buy homes, and build generational wealth at a rate on par with White families. Mckinsey released a sobering stat in a recent report: Black Americans can expect to earn up to one million dollars less than White Americans over their lifetimes. There is a laundry list of structural inequities in place that creates this gap, but the one which stands out most to me is that Black children are set up to have limited lifetime earnings due to forty-five percent of them attending high-poverty schools. Being brought up in these types of schools reduces their chances of graduating from high school and going to college, both of which are important ways to grow earning power. To contextualize this, as of 2017, only twenty-four percent of the Black population over the age of twenty-five-years-old in the U.S. has a bachelor's degree or higher. Black people in the labor market are also twice as likely to become unemployed than their White counterparts. This is true regardless of level of education, length of employment, and the cause of unemployment. We must ask ourselves, does the prospect of a Black person earning a million dollars less in their lifetime than a White person help or hurt our economy? The obvious answer is it hurts the economy, which is why, at the very least, we should all care about this, regardless of our racial backgrounds.

Companies must make racial pay equity a chief priority. Typically, there is fear around this idea because of the possibility of getting sued. But we need boards of directors and CEOs to be brave and do the work anyway. They must overcome their disclosure discomfort. Otherwise, this structural inequity will persist. At some point in the future, it will become mandatory for businesses to release this information to the public. It is better for them to get ahead of this and be seen as leaders than laggards forced to comply. Once a few brave companies put their neck on the line, other companies will follow suit and create a critical mass. Pay audits need to be conducted and companies need to follow the recommendations that come out of those. These pay audits examine racial, ethnic, and gender pay differences yearly.

Organizations then need to be transparent about those pay audits with employees, the recommendations found within them, and the gaps that exist. And since employers must file EEO-1 forms every year with the Equal Opportunity Commission, they can easily publish pay data broken down by race, ethnicity, and gender across the organization's job categories. Such transparency could clearly show where pay inequity is taking place. Overtime, it can show how a company is progressing toward closing the gap. Companies such as Starbucks, Intel, Apple, Adobe, and Salesforce have closed the gender pay gap in the U.S. So we can see it is possible. It takes time, dedication, investment, and transparency."

Derek paused to take a sip of water before continuing to his final point. "Finally, I want to lay out why investment is important to closing the racial wealth gap. The Black community has been underinvested-in for centuries. To add insult to injury, thriving Black communities such as Greenwood, Oklahoma, were destroyed or stolen. If we go back even further in our history, the labor force which was used to build much of this country was never compensated, or that compensation was just enough to scrape by.

Now, we are moving into a phase of the race conversation in which we are asking, *how do we invest in Black Americans, the descendants of enslaved Africans, in order to make them whole?* We don't have to look far to uncover what really works. If we look at White wealth in the U.S., business ownership has been a cornerstone of that wealth. The access to cheap capital creates an opportunity for sustained business operations, and these business owners are able to hand down the business through successive generations. I believe this kind of entrepreneurship is one of the key vehicles of liberation for people of color, and for Black people in particular. Entrepreneurship is a means by which communities provide value to the world, and they, in turn, are rewarded by the world for that value.

As I close today, I want to cast a vision of what investment in Black people in America can look like. Imagine that a collective of some of the largest businesses in the U.S. came together and said, 'We want to get serious about making racial equity a priority, especially for Black Americans and other racial groups who have been marginalized. But instead of just writing a check, we want to do the deep work of creating an ecosystem that will build generational wealth for centuries to come.' The leaders of these companies would learn to do business with Black-owned businesses. This is a prime way to invest in Black Americans while also contributing to a company's bottom line. However, we are aware that many Black owned businesses may not be ready to scale their services and products to the level necessary to secure significant contracts. This is not the case for all Black owned businesses, but it is for so many. Imagine if that business collective knew it was not the fault of Black businesses who find themselves in this situation, and they understood that Black people are often denied loans and access to capital needed to scale. So, the dedicated CEOs of this collective could come up with a plan to partner with prominent chambers of commerce in large cities across the U.S. to launch business accelerator programs to help strengthen the smaller, Black-owned businesses. Not only that, the collective could reach out to local nonprofits who specialize in teaching Black children and teenagers how to become entrepreneurs so that perhaps, one day, they build enterprises the larger companies want to do business with. These CEOs could make a commitment to invest one hundred billion dollars over four years for the purpose of investing in Black owned businesses, whether that be through funding these accelerator programs, creating opportunities to contract with Black businesses, or working with the entrepreneurial education non-profits. These CEOs could use their influence to get a few large banks, credit unions, and Community Development Financial Investment (CDFI) firms on board to figure out how to get affordable capital to the businesses in the accelerator programs.

A large portion of the funds these big companies set aside would go to the accelerator programs to provide small, Black-owned businesses with enough funds to grow. This accelerator program is unique because it isn't requiring Black-owned businesses to get certifications to prove they are minority-owned. This would cut some of the red tape that many Black owned companies must get past before they are allowed to do business with larger firms. Instead, the large companies would place importance on scalability, revenue, and sales, just like they would any other business.

For Black-owned businesses who are not ready to go through traditional banks, the CDFI could step in to provide the small business with the capital necessary to ramp-up operations and position themselves to work with traditional lenders. I should add that the loans CDFIs could give to Black-owned businesses would be low interest, since the money the larger companies park in the accelerator programs guarantees the contracts for Black-owned companies within an 18-month period, as those companies scale their operations. There could also be a stipulation that these Black-owned businesses must spend at least twenty-five percent of their money from the accelerator funds with other Black-owned businesses. The purpose of all this is to put a mechanism in place for generational wealth building. Let me connect all these dots for you: "First, large companies decide to invest in Black-owned businesses by earmarking billions of dollars for that sole purpose. They also partner with programs that teach children and teenagers how to run their own enterprises and/or gain the skills necessary to work for these types of companies. In this way, larger companies create a pipeline for their future suppliers and workforce.The accelerator program exists to help Black-owned businesses grow, both through technical support, access to capital, and matchmaking between the Black-owned businesses and the larger companies."CDFIs are in place to provide low-interest-capital to Black-owned businesses who cannot go through traditional lenders yet. CDFIs are willing to do this because the larger companies have guaranteed there will be contracts for these businesses once they have completed the accelerator program and can provide their services and goods at the scale required. Banks and traditional lenders will be ready to step in once Black-owned businesses grow their operations to the level needed to be "bank-ready."

Black-owned businesses who access any of the available capital flowing through the accelerator program will then direct twenty five percent percent of their business spending to other Black-owned businesses.

As a side bar, one that deserves its own space, these large companies could contract with a handful of successful Black owned businesses in their regions that are ready to scale, as the smaller Black owned businesses develop. If a larger Black owned business is at $10 million annual revenue, the conversation among the CEOs in support of investing in Black owned businesses should be how do we get them to 50 million?

This is the key to building generational wealth in the Black community. This is also an example of how we can create sustained change. We must move the conversation about race to actions that lead to equitable outcomes. This is the work I've given my life to, and the reason I almost lost it today. Some of you might ask why I focused most of my talk today on Black people and Black-owned business. Aside from me literally having skin in the game, Black people, in all of our brilliance and creative splendor, are still at the bottom rung of the social and economic ladders in this country. By lifting up Black Americans, we will lift up all racial groups who have been disenfranchised, marginalized, and kept from opportunity, including White people.

As we address that elephant in the room, we must remember to get deep enough into the weeds of systemic inequity on the basis of race to have a real shot at reshaping our nation, making it a place where all people can thrive. Thank you for your time today."

The crowd stood, giving Derek a standing ovation. Pamela stepped up beside him at the podium as the crowd continued to applaud him. She gave him a deep, heartfelt hug. Of everyone in the room, he felt she understood just how much he had to overcome to deliver the keynote. She grabbed his hand and raised it up as a referee would raise the hand of a boxer who had just won their fight.

Derek stepped back, eager to take his seat. He wiped a few tears from his eyes. He hadn't cried this much in a long time, but he realized that his truth, the truth of being a Black man in America, hit him with its full weight at that moment. He'd experienced racism in its most primal form and addressed a crowd of hundreds of people as an expert in his field, all in the same day. It was unreal.

Derek knew he had crossed a new threshold in his life that afternoon. He'd experienced a series of defining moments that would change him forever. He would never be the same again. He didn't even care what lay in store for him at Innovative Energy anymore. However things turned out, he had solid faith that he would be okay. If he survived what he experienced at the summit, he could make it through anything and come out on top. He smiled to himself as he thought about how bright his future was.

As Derek sat in his chair, he stared at the huge elephant replica in the center of the room. He hoped he did his part to advance the conversation about race in America. He was in a rare state of bliss until his contemplation was interrupted by an older White woman.

"Derek, I just wanted to tell you that you moved me today. Your speech was powerful and impactful. You are so articulate."

Derek's blood boiled immediately. *Did this old bitch just call me articulate?* he thought to himself. He let it go. He gave a tight-lipped smile and said, simply, "Thanks. You are, too."

The woman, looking puzzled, smiled and walked away. Pamela was at the podium, closing the summit out and giving her closing remarks.

DEBRIEFING

Pamela asked each of the facilitators and speakers to come back to the green room after the event for a debrief. This was a tradition she held after every summit. She felt the facilitators, speakers, her team, and she could learn a lot through sharing what they observed throughout the day.

Everyone gathered in the green room and sat in the chairs, which formed a circle in the center of the room. Pamela kicked off her Louboutin Red Bottom pumps in favor of some Gucci flip flops. Derek saw this as her signifying this was a chill space and he imagined her feet were hurting after a long day. Zhang, Sayen, Kevin, Derek, Fatima, Alex, James, Sydney, and Liz all looked at Pamela as they settled into their seats.

"Before we dive in, I want you all to know this is an authentic space where you can be vulnerable and transparent."

Before she could continue, a tall, muscular, able-bodied Black man who looked like a former secret service agent came into the green room. He walked over to Pamela and whispered something in her ear. She nodded her head and thanked him. He walked out immediately. The facilitators looked at each other in bewilderment.

"I just got confirmation that any further threat from the Brotherhood has been handled and the premises have been adequately secured. Each of you will have a personal security guard escort you to your vehicles and then follow you for up to ten miles, to ensure your safety," said Pamela.

There were sighs of relief from the entire group. Some said, "thank you," and "thank God." Derek, still upset about his experience with the Brotherhood, thought to himself, *sure, now security shows up. I don't need them. I can handle myself.*

"Ok, where were we?" asked Pamela. "As I said, this is an authentic space and I want you to share what the day was really like for you. What was your experience?"

A long pause followed as each person thought about the question. It had been a heavy day. Having the Race Conversation Summits were typically mentally and emotionally draining. When Derek saw that everyone was reluctant to speak first, he spoke up.

"For me, today drove home how far we have to go to realize racial equity in this country."

Derek could feel everyone focused on him. He took a moment to gather his thoughts, then continued. "From the moment I walked into this building, I felt challenged on every side. I experienced both microaggressions and macroaggressions, and I even had to face my own shortcomings when I was presented with the opportunity to be an ally to Liz. Racial equity work is tricky, because not only do we have to focus on outward systems, practices, and behaviors, but racial equity work, if it is truly to be transformative, forces us to look in the mirror and do the difficult internal work of being honest with ourselves. Often, we don't make time to reflect on why we make the decisions we do when it involves people with different skin color than ourselves.

I felt this war within me even as I stood toe-to-toe with the Brotherhood outside. I realized in that moment that the matrix of racism cast over our nation, which I contend with daily, has produced internal trauma I simultaneously contend with. This is absolutely taxing on my soul. And this, I argue, is how many other Black people feel. This trauma can cause us to make choices that are not in line with our best interest, that can further perpetuate a destructive cycle. How does one break free from it?

In my estimation, there are two answers to this. Better yet, the answers are two sides of the same coin: personal accountability and cultural accountability. When it comes to personal accountability, I must take ownership of my actions and the way I conduct myself in the world regardless of the level of oppression I face in this country. Doing the work of personal accountability from this standpoint is extremely difficult, and unfair, but it is the reality of what must be done to have any chance of surviving as a Black person in the United States.

I have hope that the environment will change if enough people take on this mindset, although there is a slim chance of that happening. Major systemic change only comes at a great sacrifice. And unfortunately, this is a sacrifice the White racist paradigm has proven it is unwilling to make. I'm not saying there aren't White people who haven't broken free from this paradigm and have moved toward enlightenment, but the system itself is fueled by individuals, groups, and organizations who either choose to ignore the reality of racism or actively push its agenda.

Cultural accountability has to do with the rules, regulations, and processes that Black people use to govern ourselves in light of a racist paradigm. This is not to say that the racist paradigm should color all aspects of our existence, but it should inform it. The racist paradigm impacts our survival. Groups who have been historically disenfranchised and oppressed, specifically Black people, must have our own customs and governance within the racist systems we find ourselves in. We must promote those within our culture who embody customs that promote the wellbeing and continuation of our people. And our culture must discipline those who break those customs."

"Wait, wait, wait, that sounds a bit cultish," James interjected. "Who decides what these customs are? And how do you even know if this is the right approach to solving systemic racism?"

"This is far from a cult. This approach offers a layer of protection that the Black community used to have but no longer really exists. At one point, our communities were policed by us, served by us, and uplifted by us. We've gotten away from that because of various strategies engineered by White supremacists. And the cycle of short lived progress continues. We got comfortable after the Civil Rights Era and didn't keep applying pressure to force more systemic change. As a result, Black people have regressed, despite our symbolic progress. What I'm advocating for here is what every other racial group has: a system of governance, whether formal or not."

James just shook his head. "I think you've been through a lot today, young man. We'll just have to agree to disagree."

"James, why don't you share your point of view since it is different from Derek's?" Pamela chimed in. "Perhaps your point of view offers a better solution. I also think it's beneficial to allow differences of opinion to emerge within the same racial groups."

"Okay, here's the thing," James responded. "What you are proposing, Derek, sounds a lot like Black Wall Street in the Greenwood District of Tulsa, Oklahoma. For those who don't know their history, Black Wall Street was an independent and bustling Black city back in the early 1920s. There, Black people had their own stores, banks, schools, law firms, doctors, etcetera.

What African Americans built there was powerful, and it wasn't even a hundred years after slavery ended. Black people there were so successful and independent that they made one fatal mistake. They didn't realize how vulnerable they were and how much White society despised their progress. White society looked for any reason to burn that city to the ground, which they eventually did in the Tulsa Race Massacre of 1921. All that was founded and controlled by Black people, all they labored to create in Tulsa, was destroyed within a few days.

As I listen to you Derek, I see you have the spirit of the pioneers of the Greenwood district in Tulsa. But it sounds like you are making the same mistake they did: not realizing how vulnerable you and our entire race are; and not considering that there is still an undercurrent in White society, not strong but still present, which despises all we've managed to achieve, symbolic or not.

I do think you are the caliber of leader who can establish a feat similar to that of Black Wall Street in these modern times, I just wouldn't want to see you and those you lead be met with the same fate."

The room was so quiet you could hear a spider descending its web. Many in the room were shocked to hear such a transparent and public conversation between two Black men. They were witnessing two generations of thought colliding. No one else wanted to offer their two cents. Derek guessed they felt it wasn't their place. Except for Pamela.

As Derek formed his response to what James had said, his frustration visible to all, she interjected.

"Derek, before you respond, take in everything James said to you. Not only what you feel are sharp criticisms."

Taking Pamela's advice, Derek gave himself time to think before he responded. He realized James wasn't necessarily against his ideas, he was cautioning him. James wasn't as far removed from the tragedy that occurred during the Tulsa Race Massacre as Derek. Derek heard fear in James' response, probably based on James' knowledge and experience with the aftermath of the tragedy .

Derek, on the other hand, experienced his own rendition of the racist violence committed against his ancestors during his tangle with Brotherhood earlier that day. It felt as if the ancient strife between these two groups was manifesting in the bodies walking the earth now.

As thoughts swirled in his head, Derek simply responded, "Maybe you're right, James. Actually, more than likely, you are right. But when has playing it safe ever gotten our people any further?"

Derek got up, grabbed his coat, and waived at everyone as he walked out of the green room. He was exhausted and didn't have anything left to give today. And quite honestly, those last words he spoke to the group were enough. He knew he'd left the group stunned with his departure, but he had spoken his truth. When did playing it safe ever get Black Americans any further? It never had.

As Derek exited the building, he noticed how beautiful the sun looked as it began to set behind the downtown architecture. He took his time walking to his car. His wi-fi finally kicked in and his phone started buzzing, notifying him of several missed calls and messages. One was from the CEO of Innovative Energy. Derek immediately called his voicemail to hear the message.

"Hey Derek, this is Todd. I've been trying to reach you. I know you had to speak at the summit today. I hope it went well. Hey, look,

I met with the board today and I wanted you to hear this from me before anyone else reached out. The board has recommended we promote you. The rationale is that you've been incredibly effective in your role, even in the midst of, well, lets just say... large challenges. The promotion comes at my urging, but it was virtually unanimous, which is pretty rare for our board. You are now Senior Vice President of People and Culture. This is a new title, but your influence within the company will be greatly expanded. Oh, and your office is now next to mine. We'll talk more about it in person, on Monday. I just wanted to give you the good news after what I'm sure has been a long day. Talk to you soon."

Derek stood in the middle of the parking lot, smiling. It was more than a physical smile. His soul was smiling. He put his things into the trunk of the car, opened his door, sat down, and yelled loud and long, at the top of his lungs. He felt a mix of triumph, pain, joy, and sadness all commingling in his body. He let his head relax against the soft leather of the headrest, closed his eyes, and breathed out.

THE FUTURE OF CONVERSATIONS ABOUT RACE

Hi, this is Philip, the author of the book you just read. I hope you enjoyed it. I thought it was important to close this book with parting thoughts about the style and narrative direction I took, as well as my thoughts on the future of conversations about race.

I decided to write a parable on the topic of race because it is a difficult subject and I find people are more open to discussing it if the content is entertaining, as well as thought provoking. Now, there are specific tactics the characters in the book use, which are useful in real life. My hope is you can see yourself in some of the characters as they struggled to have difficult conversations, spoke about their own experiences, and navigated the many complexities that discussions about race bring up.

As a Black man, my lived experience is the common thread throughout this book (hence the heavy emphasis on Black people and our liberation). I did research on the experiences of other racial groups and did my best to capture these experiences, though I'm aware that to some, I may have fallen short. This is an outcome I choose to live with for the initial publication of this book. Perhaps a deeper dive into the history and present experiences of other racial groups will find its way into the second edition, if there is one.

The point I hope is not lost, though, is that there is tremendous power in having conversations about race, and those conversations are not optional anymore if we hope to continue to make progress, as a society. Some would say we've had enough conversations about race and we need to take action. While I agree that the latter is of utmost importance, I also believe it is not as easy to do without the former.

Effective conversations can be life changing, especially if those conversations are consistent. There is creative power in our words and they have the ability to influence behavior, shift attitudes, and transform mindsets. All of this is necessary for anti-racism to take root in our nation and abroad.

Those pursuing racial equity have a formidable challenge on their hands. Virtually all of American industry and institutions (at least those which have been around for fifty years or more) have a bedrock of racism built into them. That racism is part of systems which self-perpetuate on auto-pilot. Awareness of such systems begins the process of disrupting them, but long term strategies must be enacted to close the dam, hopefully for good.

The fact of the matter is that people don't change easily, even when they have good intentions to do so. Pain is what produces transformation. The system of White supremacy has been set up to make its benefactors comfortable. Many of those benefactors engage in racial equity work by choice, not necessity. Which is why, in large part, changing hearts, minds, and behaviors of White people is so difficult. Many are comfortable benefactors.

What made the murder of George Floyd, and the resulting uptick in racial consciousness in the U.S., unique was the confluence of the COVID-19 pandemic, social media, and social justice protests. Had these "stars not aligned," the White supremacy system would have carried on as usual. In many ways, it already has. Yet George Floyd's death sparked a moment of discomfort in White America, even if only for a moment. Many folks, of all racial backgrounds worked and are working like hell to not lose the opportunity for forward progress which that moment wrought. I'm both discouraged and encouraged by this truth.

On one hand, I'm discouraged that it took all these forces working in concert to open just a small window of opportunity for a racial awakening to the plight of Black Americans. I'm also discouraged that a Black man's death had to serve as the catalyst. I see billions of dollars and unending multitudes of resources being poured into space travel and space accommodations, yet it is a struggle to get barely a fraction of those resources to go to deserving citizens, like George Floyd, here on earth. A good friend of mine reasoned that it's easier to colonize Mars than to achieve racial equity for Black people in the U.S.. From the looks of things, I must agree.

On the other hand, I'm encouraged because I've personally witnessed a number of people, all of whom benefit from the system of White supremacy, see the light and start doing the necessary work to disrupt the harmful effects White supremacy has on those who have been historically marginalized because of their skin color. I do think a scar was left on our nation after the murder of our dear brother, Mr. Floyd. That scar can serve as a rallying point for us to continue in the powerful but unfinished work of the Civil Rights Era. Even though racism will become more sophisticated in the future, the studs being put in place now for racial equity will make it harder and harder for those individuals and organizations who perpetuate the White supremacist paradigm to remain hidden.

I don't want to be naïve here and say that White supremacist systems are going away any time soon. They are hardwired into the fabric of this nation, therefore, I expect to see many variants of them remaining in the future (in much the same way we see variants of Covid-19 emerging today). History clearly teaches that racism adapts. We are seeing this occur in technology, politics, and wealth management, especially. Racism is an enemy that will never sit still while we do the work of digging ourselves out of this pit.

This is why people who still benefit from White supremacy, yet see it as problematic for our country, must remain vigilant about their own internal and necessary work as they actively dismantle the systems that perpetuate it. This is akin to the work Black people are required to do when they show up to their professional environments ,intent on being successful. We have to be excellent at our "regular jobs" while we simultaneously navigate both the obstacles we face internally and the White systems that oppress us. This is a dual occupation that, hopefully, future generations won't have to operate in if we do the necessary work now.

So what is this necessary work? There are quite a few elements to it, but the foundational pieces include a continuing education around how we got here. This is important because we tend to forget history, especially if it doesn't immediately affect us, and as the old saying goes, *those who fail to learn from history are subject to repeat it.* In the U.S., slavery hasn't ended. Mass incarceration is the modern manifestation of slavery, (although mass incarcertation has also been around since chattel slavery). It is important that topics like critical race theory (with a specific focus on the origins of anti-Blackness) are taught at all grade levels, including college, and are included in work/professional environments. This education must be ongoing. It does not end.

The second element of the work we must do is intentionally implement economic inclusion of Black Americans and other racial groups who have been deliberately kept out of participation in the U.S. economy, or severely hamstrung for generations. There are a variety of ways to go about this. A few include initiatives by large, White-owned or controlled companies to directly contract with Black-owned businesses for services and products they regularly utilize. If companies have a multi-billion or trillion dollar market cap, surely they can set aside a portion of their spending for the purpose of contracting with Black-owned suppliers, as well as ensure these suppliers don't have to jump through the hoops procurement departments sometimes put them through to get it.

An additional component would be Black-owned businesses, who are directly contracting with these large firms, to hold themselves accountable and spend five to twenty-five percent of their budget at other Black-owned enterprises. This should just be a part of how they do business. By making this a mandated business practice, we can ensure the practice of building generational wealth for Black Americans continues.

Policy also plays a major role in either upholding or breaking White supremacy. There are policies which limit the revenue and size of Black-owned firms if they hope to compete for government contracts. There are laws which are supposedly designed to help minority-owned businesses, to include Black-owned businesses, but in actuality they have the opposite effect by keeping minori-ty-owned businesses small. Yet we must think big if we are to ever see something like a Black-owned Nike. Shout out to what Kanye West (pardon me, I mean Ye) is doing with his Yeezy sneaker and various apparel ventures. If we want to see bigger things for Black

America and other racially oppressed groups, we must think bigger and have, or create, space to do so.

There is no doubt that we are now living in the future. With the rise of the metaverse, the race to colonize space, artificial intelligence, and proliferation of digital currency, we are officially in the Jetsons age, minus the flying cars (though I suspect those will come within the next week). So what is the future of race conversations in this context? From an aspirational perspective, I see metrics and data playing a heavy role in how race is discussed. I expect that race related metrics will be developed, used, and mandated. You can't change what you don't measure. I expect that accountability across all societal institutions and companies will be the norm, no longer the exception. At some point, the entire justice system will be turned on its head, either through innovation or scandal related to a watershed racial issue, and the justice system will be reconfigured like never before. White supremacy will find a way to rebound, but it will not be as overt as it once was in this particular system. It would be too risky due to the collective consciousness. But, new ways to marginalize will emerge if we are not careful. And given humankind's past, this new mass marginalization is more than likely to occur, reestablishing itself in the place of the old structure.

Conversations about race will not become easier in the future. Our understanding of the dynamics at play will, though, and society will become adept in utilizing more nuanced terminology when discussing race. But as long as systems exist which oppress others due to their skin color, and as long as there is no significant recompense to those who have suffered for centuries as a result, these conversations stand to become more difficult. If large organizations and high profile leaders continue to make pledges to do their part to end systemic racism in the arenas they influence, but don't demonstrate significant progress in a reasonable length of time, these conversations will not become easier.

Racial conversations have the ability to become transformative, though. That potential will be realized when White people don't rely on Black people and other people of color to provide them with education on how to be anti-racist. When White people do the work of relentlessly examining their own biases and race-related issues become just as much a part of their consciousness as people of color, the needle of progress can move significantly.

Conversations about race are not only two-way, but can be singular, as well. Black people constantly have the race conversation by themselves. We must make calculations and weigh the risks of showing up as we are every time we open our mouths in White-operated or owned establishments. When we become successful in these types of enterprises, we ask ourselves, "Am I Black enough?" So much of our experience revolves around our Blackness, whether we want it to or not.

The question in the larger conversation becomes, *can I exist as I am without my race having to be the focal point of my identity?* In the majority of spaces, unfortunately, the answer is no. But hopefully, this answer evolves to maybe, and eventually, yes, as more people across the racial spectrum are compelled to have the race conversation within.

I'm a pragmatic optimist. On one hand, I believe human hearts and minds can be changed. On the other, I realize these changes most often only occur through some sort of pain, as I mentioned earlier. What scale of pain would it take to break down the fortresses and strongholds of racism and White supremacy in the U.S.? I don't have an answer. I simply pray the answer does not have to stem from the destruction of more Black bodies.

CHARACTER PROFILES

The purpose of these character profiles is to give readers a deeper understanding of the characters within the book, in the hopes of facilitating deeper and more nuanced conversations about the characters and situations presented. The topics of race and racism in the U.S. are undoubtedly complex, and each of the characters presented here come with their own experiences and perspectives, causing them to navigate the dynamics of race in unique ways, even when they share similar racial backgrounds with other characters. These profiles are mirrors and microcosms of the people we live, learn, work, worship, and spend time with. Let their diverse backgrounds and perspectives remind you of how we each approach race/racism differently when we interact with our social circles.

Alex

Social status based on race: HIGH
Education: BA in Sociology
Net worth: $150k

Background: Alex grew up in a traditional, all-White, middle class neighborhood. She has always had a natural curiosity about cultures different from her own. She dated a Polynesian man while she was in college and doing so opened her eyes to the ways he and other people of color experience the world. She did research on the history of racial inequity in the U.S. and has been on a mission to open the eyes of other White people, specifically other White women, to the ugly realities of racism and the role they need to play in solving problems they and their ancestors created.

Derek Blain

Social status based on race: LOW
Education: MBA in Organizational Leadership from Historically Black College or University (HBCU)
Net worth: $500K

Background: Derek Blain is a young, driven, hotshot executive. He is diplomatic, yet not afraid of conflict. He was raised in a large, fast-paced city. Derek was a college and high school athlete. He welcomes competition. As a young boy, he was taught not to run from a fight and to never accept or show defeat.

Fatima

Social status based on race: MEDIUM (within the U.S.)
Education: MS in Engineering and MA in Sociology
Net Worth: $300k

Background: Fatima was born in Sri Lanka, India, where she lived until she was twelve years old, before immigrating to the U.S. with her family. She was born into the Dalit caste, the lowest social group of the Hindu caste system. Her father was a brilliant inventor who created a water purifier system using common materials that helped save his and other surrounding villages during a severe drought in the region. In a stroke of good fortune, news of his accomplishment spread throughout the region, ultimately reaching global news outlets after researchers from a prominent university traveled to his village to see his invention in person. After that, Fatima's family was granted approval to live in the U.S. Fatima attended some of the best schools, became a software engineer, and eventually transitioned into DEI work. Seeing and feeling the effects of her caste systems as a child gave her a passion for uplifting marginalized communities later in life.

Isaac (Brotherhood leader)

Social status based on race: HIGH
Education: Certificate in Auto Mechanics
Net worth: $50K

Background: The Brotherhood leader grew up in a small town on the edge of a larger city, during the 1960's, where he experienced segregation first-hand. He also experienced integration when his once all-White neighborhood began to diversify. His father was a staunch racist who moved his family out of the neighborhood soon after integration began, to an area where he was certain "good ol' fashioned lynchings" were still occuring. He vividly remembers conversations in which his father and others claimed White people were "the salt of the earth and God's only way to redeem the planet." He studied books about Hitler and the Third Reich that his father left around the house.He grew to love Hitler's ideology.

James

Social status based on race: LOW
Education: PhD in Engineering
Net Worth: $3M

Background: James is a retired executive vice president for a large global manufacturing company. James' family came from humble beginnings. Because of that, his father and mother instilled a strong work ethic in him, as well as an understanding of the importance of saving and investing money. From these foundational lessons, James took a traditional route toward success. He went to college, earned a PhD in engineering, and got a "good job" at the local manufacturing plant. He worked his way up the ladder over a thirty-year career, becoming the highest ranking African American in the company. He was wise with income, participating in the company's 401K-matching program, and he made a few investments in real estate before his hometown was gentrified. The properties he owns have nearly tripled in value since he bought them. James believes in and embodies the American Dream, but is still aware of the many inequities that Black Americans face in the US. Though retired, he spends the majority of his time as an independent DEI consultant.

Judy (disgruntled White woman at Brotherhood rally)

Social status based on race: HIGH
Education: High School dropout
Net Worth: < $10K

Background: Judy became a teenage mother at the age of fourteen, then left high school to care for her child, as a result. Her mother and father were both alcoholics and berated and shamed her daily. She moved out of her family home when she was just sixteen to escape their abuse. She lived as a single mother and supported her child by working evenings. It broke her heart to watch her friends graduate high school and go off to college without her. Now in her mid-forties, she is bitter at the lack of opportunity she continues to face. She associates many of her struggles with the amount of non-White people moving into the country and "taking all the good jobs."

Keisha

Social status based on race: LOW
Education: BA in Human Resource Management
Net worth: $105K

Background: Keisha Wilson grew up in a rough neighborhood, but her mother, father, and two older brothers shielded her from many of the negative aspects young Black women in her neighborhood faced while growing up. She was always involved in extracurricular activities at school. There, she developed a love for learning about different cultures and longed to travel the world. Her passion for Human Resources Management emerged after she interned at one of the largest companies in her city. While working there, she saw the gut wrenching effects that racism has on Black and Latino people in the workplace. Keisha has seen several DEI initiatives come and go. She wants to be a part of lasting change on local and national levels. She aspires to be mayor of her city.

Kevin

Social status based on race: HIGH
Education: Master's in Public Policy from an Ivy League university
Net worth: $5M

Background: Kevin is a former politician who now works as an independent consultant. When he saw firsthand the hidden but rampant racism within the political arena, he couldn't stomach it. He spent the rest of his political career pushing for legislation to dismantle White supremacy. His peers became his opposition until he finally decided to quit politics. Kevin grappled with his own White privilege and the history of his family, who once owned enslaved Africans, throughout his career. He now writes, speaks, and advises on how to eradicate racism and put anti-racist systems into place.

Laura

Social status based on race: LOW
Education: MBA in Marketing Communications
Economic status: $180K

Background: Laura has always had a passion for building bridges and connecting people. She is the middle-child of seven siblings. An eternal optimist, Laura is always able to find the good in people and situations, though she is not naive. She has dedicated her career as a marketing communications specialist to dismantling systemic racism in the marketing and advertising industry.

Lindsey

Social status based on race: MEDIUM
Education: Law Student at Harvard University
Net Worth: > $10k

Background: Lindsey is a Japanese American woman who is a strong ally to the Black Lives Matter (BLM) movement. She had a personal epiphany watching the mistreatment of Black people in the U.S. and over time, realized the liberation of other marginalized groups in the U.S. is inherently tied to that of Black Americans. With this new understanding, she convinced her friends to start a subset of BLM on her campus, called Asians for Blacks. She is a visible member of local BLM rallies and protests.

Liz

Social Status based on race: LOW
Education: BS in political science from state-level university
Net worth: $25K

Background: Liz Herrera is a recent college graduate. She is from humble means. She has a thirst for knowledge, truth, and curiosity about other cultures. She is a passionate disciple of Pamela Harris and works full-time as a project coordinator for Having the Race Conversation, Inc. She speaks her mind, is always authentic, and is an empathetic advocate for people who have been marginalized. She aspires to be an author and public figure.

Pamela Harris

Social status based on race: LOW
Education: MBA and PHD in Economic Policy from an Ivy League university
Net worth: $2M

Background: Pamela Harris is a seasoned, corporate veteran in her mid-fifties. She is a strategic genius with the spirit of an activist, which she inherited from her father (who was a high-ranking Black Panther party member). Pamela was a track star in high school, earning her a full-ride scholarship to an Ivy League school. Following her schooling, she began a 25-year career in corporate America as an HR professional. She was one of the highest ranking Black women in corporate America and worked for a Fortune 500 company until she became disgusted by the racist corporate machine. She then started her own company to fight against racism, Having the Race Conversation, Inc. She is a highly sought-after thought leader on race relations around the world.

Sayen

Social status based on race: LOW
Education: High School degree, Certificate in Conflict Management, and some college.
Net worth: $30K

Background: Sayen is a modern day freedom fighter. She has spent the last decade advocating for the rights of Native people. A brilliant strategist (she was often the smartest in her classes) and a passionate soul who doesn't hold her tongue for anyone, she spends the majority of her money advancing causes that positively impact her people.

Stacey

Social status based on race: MEDIUM
Education: U.S. Marines Corps Medic
Net Worth: $75K

Background: Stacey is a bi-racial woman from New Orleans, Louisiana, who relocated away from her hometown after Hurricane Katrina. She is a military veteran, serving as a medic in the Marine Corps for eight years. She strongly identifies as a Black Woman despite almost passing for White (due to her light skin tone). She also embraces being bi-racial. She is married with three kids and has strong emotional intelligence, which she credits to being the middle child of seven siblings.

Zhang Wei

Social status based on race: MEDIUM
Education: BS in Cyber Security
Net Worth: $1M

Background: Zhang was born in China, but has spent much of his life in the U.S.. He is the owner of a small and successful cyber security company. Zhang appeared to be on easy street until the tragic death of his wife of three years, due to suicide. After this tragic loss, Zhang sought deeper meaning in his life, no longer satisfied solely by earning a high income. This led to him being involved with DEI work. He is new to DEI but committed to the work, and to the process of learning to honor the memory of his wife by helping other Asian Americans who may be suffering the effects of racism.

BIBLIOGRAPHY

Blay, Zeba, Gray, Emma, "Why we need to talk about White Feminism," *Huffington Post*, August 10, 2015, https://www. huffpost.com/entry/why-we-need-to-talk-about-white-feminis m_n_55c8ca5ce4b0f73b20ba020a

Chang, Ailsa; Intagliata, Christopher; Mehta, Jonaki, "Black Americans And The Racist Architecture Of Homeownership," *NPR*, May 2021, https://www.npr. org/sections/codeswitch/2021/05/08/991535564/ black-americans-and-the-racist-architecture-of-homeownership

Community Capital Management. "Addressing the Black Homeownership Gap in America." Feb. 2021. https:// wildecapitalmgmt.net/wp-content/uploads/2021/06/

CCM-Report-Addressing-the-Black-Homeownership-Gap-in-America-Feb-2021-FINAL.pdf

Connley, Courtney, "Starbucks has closed its pay gap in the U.S.—here are 4 other companies that have done the same," CNBC, March 23, 2018, https://www.cnbc.com/2018/03/23/5-companies-that-have-reached-100-percent-pay-equity-in-the-u-s.html

Flowers, Lenon, "Is Dialogue Enough to Bridge Racial Divides?" *Greater Good Magazine,* February 1, 2021, https://greatergood.berkeley.edu/article/item/is_dialogue_enough_to_bridge_racial_divides

Gallagher, Kate, "Strategies for Closing the Achievement Gap," *TeachHub.com*, December 29, 2020, https://www.teachhub.com/teaching-strategies/2020/12/strategies-for-closing-the-achievement-gap/

Grabmeier, Jeff, "How to close the racial achievement gap," The Ohio State University, College of Education and Human Ecology, November 2017, https://ehe.osu.edu/news/listing/how-close-racial-achievement-gap

Gramlich, John, "Black imprisonment rate in the U.S. has fallen by a third since 2006," *Pew Research Center,* May 6 2020, https://www.pewresearch.org/fact-tank/2020/05/06/share-of-black-white-hispanic-americans-in-prison-2018-vs-2006/

Hayes, Adam, "Redlining," *Investopedia*. October 21, 2021. https://www.investopedia.com/terms/r/redlining.asp

Hobson, Mellody, "Color blind or color brave?" *TED2014*. March 2014. https://www.ted.com/talks/mellody_hobson_color_blind_or_color_brave

Noel, Nick; Pinder, Duwain; Stewart, Shelley; Wright; Jason, "The Economic Impact of Closing the Racial Wealth Gap," *McKinsey & Company*, August 2019, https://www.mckinsey.com/industries/public-and-social-sector/our-insights/the-economic-impact-of-closing-the-racial-wealth-gap

PBS. "Native America." October 2018. https://www.pbs.org/native-america/home/

Sue, Derald Wing; Spanierman, Lisa. *Microaggressions in Everyday Life.* Wiley, 2020.

Urban Wire. "Housing and Housing Finance," February 2019, https://www.urban.org/urban-wire/topic/housing-and-housing-finance

Beth and Jamarl. "Black husband interviews White wife on racism," *Beth and Jamarl*, June 25, 2020, https://www.youtube.com/watch?v=3yObFHMImLg

i-D. "Real Life as a Young and Native American," *i-D*, April 10, 2019, https://www.youtube.com/watch?v=uINNLzc3Kcw.

More Wong Fu. "Growing Up VietnameseAmericans," *More Wong Fu*, July 23, 2020, https://www.youtube.com/watch?v=0LxNzMcUt5Q

ACKNOWLEDGMENTS

I'd like to acknowledge every person on the front lines fighting to dismantle racism in its various forms and supporting Black Americans and other people marginalized by their skin color, as we struggle to gain liberation in the U.S. and abroad.

I've had the privilege of meeting and/or listening to dozens of people who have inspired me in this work. I cannot list them all here. But I hope my writing makes you proud, all of you, and that it serves as one more straw (among many) on the "elephant's" back, doing its part to eventually deal a deathblow to the system of White supremacy.

Lastly, a huge shout out to Christina Vega and the Blue Cactus Press team for their help in bringing my concept to life in excellent fashion. I appreciate you!

ABOUT THE AUTHOR

Philip "Sharp Skills" Jacobs has been called a modern-day renaissance man. He is an entrepreneur, award-winning hip-hop artist, speaker, author, senior consultant, and inventor. He was the first Executive Director of Washington Employers for Racial Equity (WERE), a coalition of 80+ companies in Washington State committed to making the region equitable for Black Washingtonians and all people of color. Before WERE, he was lead for a DEI solution called Racially Savvy Leadership, in which he equipped executives and leaders of Fortune 500 companies to have difficult conversations about race (before the topic went mainstream in corporate culture). Philip is a distinguished alum of Seattle Pacific University, where he obtained a bachelor's degree in business administration. He was awarded the institution's prestigious Medallion Award in 2019. He holds the PMP credential in project management, is the author of several books and has independently produced numerous music albums. His proudest accomplishment is being the father of Philip Jr. and Jonathan. Philip is from Inglewood, California, and now calls Washington home.